Let's Get It!

LET'S GET IT!

10 Keys
to Building Your Nonprofit
to Maximum Impact

KRISTOFFER E. DOURA

NEW YORK

LONDON • NASHVILLE • MELBOURNE • VANCOUVER

LET'S **GET IT!**

10 Keys to Building Your Nonprofit to Maximum Impact

Published in New York, New York, by Morgan James Publishing. Morgan James is a trademark of Morgan James, LLC. www.MorganJamesPublishing.com

The opinions expressed in this book are those of the author and not necessarily those of any associated entity. It is recommended that you seek tax and/or legal advice from a tax professional or attorney. Life insurance examples shown and returns on investments may not be the same in every situation. Life insurance costs are based on the underwriting class at issue. Performance on investments is not guaranteed. 4903100RLB_Sep24

Proudly distributed by Ingram Publisher Services.

A FREE ebook edition is available for you or a friend with the purchase of this print book.

CLEARLY SIGN YOUR NAME ABOVE

Instructions to claim your free ebook edition:
1. Visit MorganJamesBOGO.com
2. Sign your name CLEARLY in the space above
3. Complete the form and submit a photo of this entire page
4. You or your friend can download the ebook to your preferred device

ISBN 9781631958939 paperback
ISBN 9781631958946 ebook
Library of Congress Control Number: 2022931801

Cover and Interior Design by:
Chris Treccani
www.3dogcreative.net

Morgan James is a proud partner of Habitat for Humanity Peninsula and Greater Williamsburg. Partners in building since 2006.

Get involved today! Visit MorganJamesPublishing.com/giving-back

DEDICATION

To my Family,

First, my dedication to writing this book is to the people who have supported my efforts and have been with me throughout my journey as an adolescent, and throughout my adult life, the support my family and friends has provided me is truly invaluable.

Mom, I love you with all my heart and your patience, love, and belief, and wisdom has strengthened my abilities and enhanced my growth and allow me to drive myself to become the best version that I can be.

Dad, I can genuinely say that having a man like you in my life inspired me to become focused, dedicated to striving in becoming a man of resilience, honorable, and to never stop myself from adapting and overcoming challenges that have strengthen my senses through the course of experience and strong will.

Caroline, my sister, you've inspired my creativity and ignited my love for music and deepened my soul in sharing with me the rhythm and soul of many different music and sounds. From pop, hip hop, classical, and jazz, I've used the rhythm and beats and sounds of music to forever guide me and inspire my creativity.

Christina, my sister, since we were teens having fun playing Nintendo and Super Nintendo video games, I've always appreciated the journey on the missions. We learn a lot about each other working together on strategy of solving problems together. You have always encouraged me to learn to grow with a team, which has helped shaped me as an adult.

I learn so much from my family members and have always known my strength comes from my family and the people who have helped me become the man I have become.

Thank you.

TABLE OF CONTENTS

CHAPTER 1

Welcome

Nearly lost in the shuffle of all the hardships suffered as COVID-19 spread like wildfire across the world in 2020 was the crushing effect that the worldwide pandemic had on nonprofit organizations. It was hard to blame people for ceasing their donations or for giving at a far smaller rate than prior to the arrival of the coronavirus. Suddenly they found themselves questioning everything about their own lives. Would they have enough to eat? Would their kids continue to get an education? Would they continue to be employed?

The first six months of the pandemic, featuring an unprecedented global lockdown on travel, gatherings, and basic human interaction, saw a precipitous drop-off in the abilities of nonprofit organizations to function as they were intended. Events by the thousand were cancelled. Keynote speakers and celebrity meet and greets were reduced to sterile Zoom calls or done away with entirely. At charities around the world, phone lines that used to ring all day fell silent. Some nonprofit offices were shuttered entirely, with their brain trusts and volunteers working from home, trying to figure out new strategies and techniques to keep donations coming in and love and care going out. By the end of 2020, a poll of nonprofit leaders revealed that 64 percent had cancelled fundraising events directly due to the pandemic, 45 percent had lost funders or corporate partners, and 31 percent were at risk of losing grants or contracts with government agencies.[1] In the United States, 2020 was a year of big shifts in the way people thought and how their actions and words moved together. There was the call for great social upheaval, there were riots and movements and clashes between people of different opinions that threatened to turn violent, or did, with scary results. There was a polarizing political race that looked like it might tear this great nation apart. All of those factors, combined with the unprecedented arrival of COVID-19, threatened the sustainability and success of nonprofit organizations all around the world.

My name is Kristoffer Doura, and I am professionally focused on philanthropy, specifically on helping nonprofit organizations become sustainable. I have been successful in my professional life by applying the real-life events of my upbringing, athletic career, and life beyond them both to implement strategies for nonprofits that are facing trouble with becoming sustainable, building infrastructure, and combating unprecedented challenges such as COVID-19's debilitating effect on how the world works. My personal story is a whirlwind of adventures in which I lived in the biggest city in the United States as well as a developing country growing up; how I went from being a shy kid that few people talked with to the biggest kid at school who attracted lots of attention; and how I went from zero athletic background to playing in the

---

1   Nonprofit Leadership Center, "Survey Reveals Impact of COVID-19 and 2020 Challenge on Nonprofits at Year-End," November 16, 2020, https://nlctb.org/news/survey-results-covid-19-impact-on-nonprofits/.

National Football League. And that's just the tip of the iceberg! Those experiences and others have given me exclusive insight into how teams function—and how they fail—and how great leaders inspire people to perform beyond their normal capabilities and build something truly special.

I was motivated to write this book after seeing so many non-profits struggle during 2020. While COVID-19 played a heavy hand in many of those incidents, it was not the only factor. Non-profits across the country are struggling for a number of reasons, despite most of them being well-meaning in their attempts and efforts. My expertise lies particularly in legacy planning. I am at my best when I am guiding organizations through teamwork and strategic planning. COVID-19 was the most significant disruption in the way nonprofits operate in the past century, but it won't be the last problem that we face going forward. I was able to share techniques and strategies to get several of my clients back up and running during some of the darkest times last year, but I realized it wasn't enough. If I were an independent consultant hired by Reebok to boost sales, I wouldn't be worried about how adidas and Nike are doing at the same time. But charities and nonprofit organizations are not competitors all fighting for the same dollar from every philanthropist out there. They are people seeking to build relationships and inspire people to help those in need. Even if I worked 80 hours a week, I could never help every struggling nonprofit organization shake loose of its infrastructure and other problems and be successful. But by creating a knowledge hub through this book, I have a chance to do exactly that.

I am not your typical author of a book on planning for non-profits. If you see me walk in the door of your office, there's no doubt that I'll stand out from the rest. At six feet, seven inches and built like a tank, I don't look like your typical consultant. I like that differentiation because it reflects my personality and my passion. Just like I stand out in a crowd, you'll find this book does as well. A lot of authors will send you spiraling through chapters of economic theory and the ethos of giving. That's not who I am nor is it what this book is about. I'm going to share my personal story and relate the experience and obstacles I have faced that mirror key challenges in the nonprofit environment. What you'll come away with are the skills to build an organization efficiently with your team and the knowledge of how to implement a strategic plan that allows your organization to endure a long time without dissolving.

I am specifically writing this book for the founders, CEOs, C-suite executives, and team leaders of nonprofit organizations. It does not matter if you're just starting out or if you have been in business for 50 years, these lessons transcend any time period. The COVID-19 pandemic has forced a lot of organizations to hit the reset button on how they are made up, how they appeal for funds, and how they deliver on their core mission goals. Regardless of whether your organization is just starting up or regrouping from the frustrations of 2020, there is ample guidance in this volume to let you envision a much brighter future. I encourage anyone in the early stages of planning or creating a nonprofit to also drink this information in. Knowledge is power.

The first sport I ever played competitively was basketball, which was in my sophomore year of high school. I was the tallest kid, but I did not have good basketball skills. I didn't know the rules, I couldn't dribble, and my coordination was not good. Some other guys on the team were more than a foot shorter than me, but they had been playing basketball all their lives and they had street skills that I lacked. I could probably clobber every single player on the team if I wanted to, but there was not a single one I could beat in a game of one on one. A lot of nonprofits have that same sort of difficulty. They might be the biggest or have the deepest pockets, but they don't have the necessary skills to be successful. Until they gain those, they'll just stumble around going through ups and downs, just like I did on the basketball court back then.

My unique experience allows me to provide content and resources that you're not going to find anywhere else. My strategic planning experience with investment and insurance products will help build your internal strategies that allow you to continue providing value to your communities and honoring the missions that got you into this line of philanthropy in the first place.

In each chapter, I will be sharing part of the journey I have gone on. A lot of these scenarios start off in the real world or in the world of sports, but allow me to teach parallels to the nonprofit world and how remarkably similar they are: the challenges, the obstacles, the networking, the growth mindset, and the resources necessary for your nonprofit to expand its scope, its connections, and its ability to provide for others.

My promise to you, the reader, is that I will share all of my tools, processes, and experiences in order to allow you to achieve sustainability and growth in these hectic, uncertain times. The nonprofit world is not one of competition, but of communion and belief that better days ahead can be reached by all of us, not just some of us. I think a lot of nonprofits felt like they had the rug pulled out from under them in 2020. They might have been cruising along, having one good year after another, and suddenly COVID-19 came out of nowhere and they were bleeding money. Events got cancelled, speakers had to say no, your silent auction became a virtual auction, the phones stopped ringing, and you had to decide whether to shut down entirely, lay off staff, or file for bankruptcy. For a lot of nonprofits, by the middle of 2020, they were feeling like life was over.

I know how that feels, perhaps better than anyone you'll ever meet. When I was playing professional football for the Miami Dolphins, I started feeling sick and I completely blacked out on the field. I don't remember being put in the ambulance, but I do remember being in it, seeing things like bridges out the window, then monitors and doctors and nurses around me. The next thing I knew there was a team of doctors around me saying that things were not looking good and that I was severely dehydrated. They had to decide what to do next because I had a serious blood clot. If they didn't perform surgery on me in a small window of time, they might have to amputate my leg. When I woke up from the surgery, I was in a hospital bed, laid out, filled with IVs, my whole family around me. When they knew I was awake, the doctors came to see me and I found that the surgery to remove the blood clot had taken about 16 hours and, at one point, my heart had suffered such a shock that I had died on the operating table.

Not figuratively, but literally. My heart stopped beating and the doctors had to restart it, or I would have stayed dead. I came back, however, and got a second chance at life. No matter how badly the COVID-19 lockdown affected your nonprofit organization, you now have a second chance to build it back, build it better, and make a difference, just like I have.

CHAPTER 2

Life Experiences

ife experiences. Everyone has them, and no two people ever share all the same ones. Your life experiences will shape the way you act, the way you think, what your belief system looks like, where your passions lie, what roles you fit into, and what motivates you to want to do more. Being able to process those experiences and grow from them is vital in any situation. They not only keep you from making the same mistakes over and over again, but they also give your perspective on how to engage with other people, how to broaden your horizons, how to add to your skill set, and how to grow beyond those experiences.

CULTURE CHANGE

My Story

My life experiences were founded in a series of culture changes that saw my family move from New York City, where I was born, to Florida, then on to Haiti, where my parents were born, and finally back to Florida, where I finished public school. I was born in Queens, New York, on April 13, 1987. I attended PS 165 and was the tallest kid in the classroom from the first day I ever went to school. Most kids could not figure out where I was from because of my complexion—sort of a mocha color. A lot of people thought I was Native American, maybe Cherokee. I found myself with lots of interests at an early age, but nothing really stuck for me as something that I would get really passionate about for a long stretch of time. I enjoyed science a lot and would place highly in our school science fairs, but I think it might have mostly been because I had a crush on my teacher! I got into music for a while and had the chance to play the violin, but I struggled with reading music. I wound up taking Tae Kwon Do for a while and enjoyed the moves and the motions of the class, but I never could commit myself to going through all the practices that were necessary to really get good. I never worried about doing what the manual said to go on to the next color of belt; I just wanted to fight.

I loved seeing the snow on the ground; it holds so many happy memories for me. I would go out and lay in it and make snow angels, or my siblings and I would have snowball wars. I had a few friends around the neighborhood and would spend time with them after school. One was a kid named Frankie who had twin older brothers and a pair of Rottweilers living at their place. Those dogs were scary, and the brothers were intimidating. I never wanted to consider what it would be like to have the brothers or the dogs after me, but when you were there hanging out with Frankie, you definitely felt safe. I imagine his family had the dogs for protection, because you would have to have a death wish to break into their place once you heard those two dogs start barking. Frankie was a rebel and always getting into trouble. He looked like the most nonchalant guy you'd ever want to meet most of the time, but he had a temper, and it would get the best of him more often than not. Eventually, Frankie and his family were evicted on account of the dogs. It was tough to see them go because we were friends, and it's hard when you're young and see one of the bitter realities of life: a family kicked out of their home and a friend you figured you would grow up with now gone forever.

When I got a little older, my father gifted me with a red bike for Christmas and that really changed the way I looked at the world. It had two grip brakes and six-speed gears. Suddenly, I was no longer plodding down the block, I was really dashing and having a great time around the entire neighborhood. It became my way of being free. There were some people on the block that weren't as nice and weren't out there to be your friend. Once was a neighbor named Bruce, who was a biker. In hindsight, I can tell you that I was emulating cool Bruce on his bike when I would go racing down the street on mine. He would honk the horn at us kids to get out of his way, and I'm not entirely certain he would have stopped if we had not.

Lots of people didn't seem to know what to make of me because of the color of my skin. It sounds pretty silly saying that to a Florida audience, where pretty much everyone is some derivative of brown, but that's not how it was where I grew up. I'm not making it up, there were some people who mistook me for a Cherokee when I was growing up. That's about the last culture on earth that makes up part of my DNA! Despite the case of mistaken identity, those were good years, the kind of times where you're having first impressions about everything. Sitting at the lunch table and exchanging ideas, talking about who had the coolest lunchbox, who was going to win the science fair; I remember building rockets out of Pepsi bottles, and someone would always build the volcano and make it "erupt" with vinegar and baking soda. Even at that early age I was interested in a form of competition, and I was a diligent student when something really caught my attention.

I had an open mind for trying new activities from a young age, and I think that's part of the reason why I've continued to learn throughout my life. I tried the violin when I had the chance as a child, and although I was very interested in it, I couldn't master the different keys. I wanted to pursue it and take lessons, and there was actually a meeting where, if you attended, you could win free lessons for the rest of the year or win a free guitar. Unfortunately, I had my judo class at the same time and couldn't make the meeting, and another kid in my class won the lessons. It was a real hard first look at keeping my commitments and something that has stuck with me ever since.

I experienced my first culture change when my parents decided to move us to Florida. One of my siblings had asthma and the cold New York weather was making it worse. At first, I was worried about that move because the big city was all I had ever known, but that attitude changed quickly once we got there. I was able to bring my bike with me and found Florida to be way more spacious and greener than New York City ever could be. We were the new family in a pre-construction neighborhood, and I started really finding myself when we got there, taking strolls and bike rides around the neighborhood and meeting new friends. We were a bunch of troublemakers once we all got together. We'd play sports, but we also did juvenile things like throwing eggs at houses and knocking on doors and then running away. When the weather was bad, we would head inside, and I got hooked on playing video games. Super Nintendo was my thing, and Mario, Star Wars, and Donkey Kong. I made friends with a guy named Clint whose family was from Trinidad, so we sort of looked alike. He lived on the opposite side of the street, and we would take our bikes and cruise around the neighborhood. We would play sports out in the street and in these big fields behind our houses. There was all this new construction everywhere, but basically, we could just go out and see for miles and miles. I'd come home after school and go outside and play with all the boys and girls in my neighborhood.

I was in elementary school, and I got put into the D.A.R.E. program when I was in fifth grade. If you haven't heard of it, it stands for the Drug Abuse Resistance Education program. I wasn't using drugs, but I was a kid who was in trouble a lot, which of course often leads to things like abusing drugs and alcohol. It was sort of a premeditated step by the school district to try and nip the problem in the bud for me and several of my friends. There were all kinds of rebellious kids in the program; we were pretty much running the rebellion against the school. A couple of my best buddies and I would just leave school and go hang out at a park, talking to girls, getting in trouble, pretty much just living by our own rules. We tried to lift one of our teachers' cars one day in the parking lot, only to realize it was a car belonging to another teacher, and we got in big trouble. I was kicked out of D.A.R.E. for attempted vandalizing and my mom had to come rescue me from the principal's office. I was getting bigger and taller all the time and realizing I was not going to be treated like a kid for very much longer when I messed around. Responsibility was headed my way and quickly.

I can't say that my behavior was the sole reason for our next move, but I'm certain it was a contributing factor. My parents were both Haitian and had been born there. They purposely had all three of their children while living in the United States but were starting to feel more and more like they wanted to go back to the island and let us see where we had come from. We left Florida for Haiti and it was the biggest culture shock of my entire life.

There's not much of a physical distance between the two; you can fly from Miami to Haiti in just about two hours, but the cultural distance between the two is staggering.

We moved to Haiti in the early 2000s, following an enormous period of turmoil in the country. There was a military coup in the late 1980s and another in 1991. Thousands of Haitians fled the country by boat to the United States, and in the mid-1990s, the United States sent troops to occupy Haiti, eventually turning it over to the United Nations.

We left our suburban Florida neighborhood and traveled to a place my parents said was home, but it felt more like a nightmare. Haiti even today struggles with basic things like water supply and sanitation. It ranks last among North American countries in the World Economic Forum's Network Readiness Index, which indicates how developed countries are in terms of information and communications technology. It also ranks 174 out of 186 countries in per-capita income.

Haiti is an island, but it really makes you feel like you're on an island, if you catch my drift. Everything was different there. The streets, the people, the environment, all of it. It was not the city life that I was used to. Miami might have had drugs and crime and gangs, but it also had the feel of the city, those beautiful palm trees, and the atmosphere that made you think something exciting was right around the corner.

Despite all those negatives, my parents were convinced that I was going down the wrong tunnel in Florida and that it was time for a change. Living in Haiti was extremely different from life in the United States. A good word for it was unregulated. It had the same type of government as the United States, but that was pretty much where the similarities ended. Things we take for granted like electricity and running water and being able to go to a McDonald's down the street—those things were not set in stone in Haiti. There weren't chains and retail stores in Haiti. Everything was locally owned and locally run. This was before Amazon and Google shopping and all of that was prevalent, so you either bought it from a local store or you had it shipped from the US, knowing full well that it might take forever to arrive, and someone might steal it off the plane, from the post office, or off the mail truck. Everything in Haiti seemed like it was moving at a much slower pace, and that was going to be a big problem for me, given that I was entering those tween years when you start questioning everybody and everything around you. Unfortunately, things weren't as slow and simple in Haiti as I was led to believe.

I remember going to school one morning in the car with my parents and seeing a dead body on the road. It was my first time seeing someone who was not alive, and it shook me up. I remember thinking, "Wow, it really is a jungle out here." The body was there for hours and hours before someone came and took it away. Everyone was just gawking at it, and you could see blood everywhere, which made me realize the person had probably been shot. There were dangerous areas of town that you knew not to go to. That had been the case in Florida, but not like this. Here, if you stayed out after dark, you weren't sure you were coming back at all. I started acting like a protector for my mom and my sisters; people were wary of me because of my size, even though I was technically still a kid. My dad was there taking care of the adult stuff, but I was the one at home and keeping an eye on things.

We attended a good school despite some of the circumstances of where we were living. It was called the Morning Star Christian Academy and we went there for sixth and seventh grade. It was a unique school in that there was not a traditional teacher and chalkboard setup. Instead, it was very largely self-taught. We had assistants, but otherwise we were moving on our own time through lots of literature, and applying it to things like religion and other parts of our education.

I'll be honest with you, if I had not been a self-starter and a perfectionist, I would have probably failed out of that school because they were not there to hold your hand, wipe your nose, pat you on the back, or tell you that it was going to be alright. You were there to get work done and if you couldn't figure it out on your own, then you were going to be moving at a snail's pace while everyone else was zipping along.

Making it for myself turned out to be exactly what I needed, and I taught myself new concepts in math, new ways of reading books, and a lot of other disciplines that propelled me forward to be an excellent student when I later returned to the United States. It was in Haiti, of all places, that I had one of my best educational experiences and a bit of racial pride to go with it.

The school in Haiti used a software program called Mavis Beacon Teaches Typing to show kids how to get comfortable with a keyboard. Even back then in Haiti, they were realizing that the future of the world was going to be on computers and in jobs that you did in an office, not in a field. Mavis Beacon was a fictional character, but she could have run for president and won in Haiti. The picture of the woman on the box was a Haitian-born lady named Renee L'Esperance, who had been discovered working at the perfume counter of a Saks Fifth Avenue in Beverly Hills and became a model. She was selected by The Software Toolworks company to represent their brand, the first female African American computer character that was used to promote learning. Her name came from a combination of the singer Mavis Staples and the word beacon, as in a guiding light.

So, imagine you are a kid growing up in Haiti and, even though you weren't born there, you know that's your heritage, and here's this computer program teaching you to type, and it's got a woman who looks a lot like you and everybody else in the classroom on the cover of the box! That was a big moment, I think, in realizing that not everyone famous was white or an athlete. That someone looking like me could make a difference in the world wherever I wanted to.

According to research, Mavis Beacon Teaches Typing is now the best-selling instructional typing software of all time, and by 1998, it was instructing six million school children around the world. The typing program was a good example of the type of education we were getting at the school. It was tough on me; you had to follow the screen and type on the keyboard, and you were constantly challenged on how many words you could type a minute, and if you didn't make the grade you went back to the start. It was a long way from life in Florida, where there had been teachers walking around helping me with instructions and answering any questions on assignments and tests.

It was at that school that I had my first experience with organized sports. My height allowed me to join the basketball team. I loved watching it on television—it was the heyday of the Chicago Bulls with Michael Jordan, Scottie Pippen, and Dennis Rodman—but I had never learned to play the game and I had very little coordination. What I did discover there are things that I have kept with me all my life—things like brotherhood, community, and a sense of organization. These were vital, irreplaceable possessions for me. I was suddenly surrounded by a group of guys I felt safe with. There was not much of a sense of community where we lived. There were situations where you might get kidnapped and ransomed back to your family. There were times when your basic needs were not going to be met by the government. My parents were having to buy things like batteries, generators, and a power source for our home to ensure we had the necessities 24/7. We had a huge house in Haiti, a three-story house with lots of land to run around on as a backyard. We had helpers, as well, who were a bit like servants, but we also could see very specifically that we didn't have it nearly as good as we had it in the United States. It took me a while to realize that the entire globe does not have a functioning economy with tools and resources like the United States did. There were times when it was really depressing living there. You couldn't just go play outside on the block with your friends, you kept on having to be careful with where you went and what you did.

Of course, it wasn't all bad memories. Nothing ever is. Even if you're in prison, you find ways to make the best of your time. You adapt and you find pleasure in things you can rely on and make those your new normal until the next change comes along and you adapt again. One of those new things for me was getting a dog—the first pet I ever had! His name was Blackie, and he was the best thing I could ever imagine. He made me so happy; I have no qualms about calling him my best friend when I was living in Haiti. I took care of him like he was my son. I'd wash him and nurture him and give him all kinds of love and affection every day. Along the way we got a second dog, a Dalmatian we named Lucky, who was a beautiful, huge dog, happy and joyful. Those two dogs became brothers and, whenever I had a bad day, the two of them would put a smile on my face. On the weekends, I'd get this huge tub out and wash them both and it would be just like a scene in a movie, the two of them going in and out of the tub, shaking off everywhere, getting everything soaking wet. Those were happy memories.

My mom eventually realized that despite our big house and servants and land, Haiti was not a good place for us. After two and a half years there, she put everything we owned up for sale to liquidate it and get some value for it. It was a big decision, but it was made easier by the fact that things in Haiti were not going well; the country was starting to unravel. When you call a place home, like my parents had, it's hard to see when the writing is on the wall because you want to believe in the place you're from. You don't want to believe that the home you grew up with is gone forever, so you manage to keep looking the other way and convincing yourself that it's not so bad. But then the kidnappings and the ransoms and the corruption just keep getting closer and closer to your front door and eventually it's right in front of you, hitting you over the head that it's not safe here anymore for your family. Being American might have afforded us a nice house, a tall fence, and a lot of servants, but it also made us into targets. We felt as if our opportunities and chances were becoming more and more limited, and that there was a lot more for us in the United States.

I can say that living through that experience and having to live through an economy where you were always uncertain what was going to happen next was an eye-opener for me. It showed me how grateful I was. When I thought about how people who have abilities are receiving benefits and welfare in the United States, I realized how truly fortunate I was even while living in a developing country. It made me realize that it didn't matter where I was at, if I were able to adapt to any situation, then I was five times stronger than if I hadn't gone through that type of experience. That taught me how to appreciate the simple things in life.

We headed for Miami, and those two and a half years that I was gone were a tough time to not be growing up with my own peer group in the United States. I wasn't up to speed with the kids my age in terms of what was popular, what was trendy, what were the clothes to be wearing and the music to be listening too. I went to an inner-city school and that was tough. I was too big for anyone to think about beating me up, but I got picked on plenty. I was this oddball kid wearing Old Navy clothes; I didn't have the cool kid clothes like FUBU. I was lacking that sense of community that I had been able to establish in Haiti. It wasn't the nicest place to live, but it had been a good school and I had gotten to know the teachers and coaches. Now I was back to being the odd man out and it took me a lot of time to figure things out.

It didn't help that the next year I would be going to high school as the low man on the totem pole. Despite my size, I was still going to be a freshman in a world full of 17- and 18-year-olds running the school. I got into wrestling as another go-round at organized sports and that helped a lot. I got back into Judo again because I thought it would help me with self-defense if I needed it. It was the same problem as before, though. I liked going to the workouts and learning to use my arms, legs, and body weight, but I didn't want to master the next belt. I found myself being an all-or-nothing guy. If I wasn't into it at a full swing, I was not doing it at all.

My school the next year was a brand-new school and a huge culture shock for me. A lot more kids than I was used to, and much older kids as well. There didn't seem to be a lot of structure my freshman year, nor a sense of control—you were just going to your classes, going to lunch, kids everywhere, no sense of purpose. That was hard for a guy like me. What was worse was that there was a strong gang presence at the school. Gangs would wear different colors and sweatpants and gangs from other schools would come to our school just to pick fights with the gangs there. Sometimes you felt like you were walking through a war zone.

I was able to make two really good friends by the time I was a sophomore, and that helped me out immensely. Having another person or two who you could use as a sounding board was exactly what I needed—really, something we all need. One of them was Robert, who sat next to me in class. He was from Cuba, which is only about 400 miles from Haiti in the Caribbean, so we were able to relate on a lot of things; our cultures were pretty similar. We would have a great time laughing and joking in class.

His family hired me to work at their restaurant at the shopping mall, and that was my first real paying job. It's been almost half a lifetime since we were in school together, but we still keep that relationship today. We had each other's backs almost from day one. There were some people in our neighborhood who either didn't like him or didn't like me, and we got in a couple of scraps, had a couple of brawls. It was just guys being guys, but we knew we could count on each other in a situation like that. It was fun more than anything. We were learning to be accountable and learning who we could rely on in life. Life in the suburbs was more of a stepping-stone for me. I was learning so much about myself and learning what it meant to be part of a community. It would take me on the path that I'm still on today.

My other friend was a guy named Michael from Colombia. He thought I was going after his girlfriend because she and I always used to talk in class, but I didn't even know they were together. Once he realized I wasn't interested in dating her, he and I became really great friends.

Teachable Moments

Culture is a term that's bandied about a lot these days in the business environment, and that goes double for the nonprofit landscape. I went through three massive culture shifts as I was growing up, bouncing from New York City to Florida, then on to Haiti and back to Miami. It's not just about geography, either. We're talking about the way of speaking, the way of communicating, what language you speak, how you carry yourself, the food, the customs, everything.

There's been a culture shift in the US and all around the world thanks to the COVID-19 pandemic. Businesses being forced to shut down—at least the ones that didn't fall under the arbitrary "non-essential" designation were forced to rethink their whole business model. If you're a movie theater owner, how do you make money when people can no longer sit next to each other to watch the next blockbuster from Marvel Studios? If you're a restaurant owner, how can you turn a profit when every other table in your once packed restaurant is now left empty to prevent the spread of germs? If you manage a department store, how do you get back in the black during Q3 each year with your back-to-school sale when about 70 percent of kids in the country aren't going back to school? And if you're a nonprofit organization that thrives on in-person events, luncheons, galas, meet and greets, and hands-on volunteering to really make that connection between the people generous to donate and the people who are most affected by their donations, what do you do when all of that goes away for months at a time?

One of the things I learned in my journey through childhood is that it doesn't matter where you're at; if you're able to adapt to any situation, you are five times stronger than you would be if you hadn't gone through any type of experience that teaches you a lesson on how to appreciate the simple things in life.

Was the COVID-19 shutdown and its ongoing limitations something terrible to endure as a nonprofit organization? Absolutely. Did it cost nonprofits across the country thousands or even millions of dollars in lost donations, not to mention planning of events? Of course, it did. But does that have to continue just because there's a new normal? Absolutely not!

Culture change is going to come to every organization, and not just because of a virus that, at the time of this writing, was approaching 500,000 deaths in the United States alone. Culture change comes in many forms, such as when a nonprofit loses or gains a powerful partner in business or government. It comes when vital staff members leave for greener pastures. It changes when there is an unfortunate scandal or bad publicity. It changes simply because change is a part of life.

The essential part of change is having staff who are adaptable. Everyone in your organization will have their set roles that they excel in, but flexibility is essential in a nonprofit. Your organization is not a massive megacorporation with so many redundancies that there are eight people in every department that have the exact same job title and tasks. You need people whose skill sets look like the living embodiment of a Swiss Army knife—a little marketing, a little copywriting, a little bit of phone skills, a little bit of accounting, etc. These are the people who are going to be the most vital to your organization during a period of massive change, as we experienced last year with COVID-19.

How Do We Adapt to Change?

We've identified the change that has gone on and we've got a staff of people who could probably do a pretty good job if we dropped them in the middle of the wilderness with nothing more than a water bottle, some beef jerky, a knife, and a sleeping bag. But what comes next? The initial steps are a lot less daunting than you might think. The first thing we need to pursue is unity. That's not to mean everyone has to have the same thought process, but it means that everyone needs to get involved. Do you know what one of the biggest fatal flaws is for traditional businesses during a time of great change? They extremely narrow the focus of who should figure out what to do next. Which means if you don't have an acronym that starts with a "C" in front of your name (CEO, CTO, CFO, etc.) or you don't have a seat on the board of directors, you are probably not going to have a single word of input into how the company should pivot now that change has come and disrupted your process.

For huge companies, that's hard to fathom. Imagine a company with 100,000 employees being vain and egotistical enough to imagine that only a dozen or so of them have the intellect and vision to decide how the company should respond. Twelve out of 100,000? That sounds about like your odds of winning the Powerball. But that's how so many businesses make their policy and go forward with the decisions that will impact millions of lives—their own, their employees, their families, their business partners, and of course, their customers.

A friend of mine from Texas, who has given me some great advice in writing this book, shared a story with me once about his time in the newspaper industry. He had started out in the business a few years before the Internet really took hold, so when suddenly everything was online, newspapers took a real hit on revenue—especially with classified ads as sites like Craigslist, Inc. took over. There were 13 newspapers in the chain he worked for, and he and the other 12 publishers were called to the company headquarters for a big meeting, at which they were told the future of the entire company had been decided by a brain trust of two people—the 83-year-old founder of the company and the 71-year-old president of the company. Let that sink in for a moment. The future of the entire organization and how it should best adapt to this new technology that was literally revolutionizing everything had been decided in a series of lunch meetings by the two oldest employees of the company. Not to say that older people don't understand the Internet, but we're talking about two gentlemen that had not worked at an actual newspaper in more than a quarter of a century! Meanwhile, the 12 publishers of the actual papers were biting their tongues and squeezing their palms in an effort to not speak up and contradict the new world order. Needless to say, the strategy was not a good one and the newspaper chain in question saw its outlets dropping like flies in the decade to come.

The myopic view that only a select few are qualified to steer a company during times of great change is not a mistake that non-profit organizations can afford to make. You need to get everyone involved; to turn a nautical phrase, you need all hands on deck. Everyone on your staff comes from different backgrounds, which means they have seen all different types of adversity. Given that they are now in your employ and have chosen to work for a non-profit, that indicates that they have not only faced adversity, but they've also overcome it. They have seen change before and have made the right moves to get past it and keep charging. When you get everyone involved, not only do you open up the discussion to every good idea that people might have, but you also do some of the best culture building that exists. You're letting every member of your staff know:

Your voice matters

We see you as a valuable resource, not just an employee

All of us together are greater than any of us on our own.

When you make everyone a part of the process, you are empowering every person who works for you with the knowledge that their ideas and insight are welcome. Even a kernel of an idea can catch flame in a group discussion and turn into something special, something that reignites your nonprofit organization's look, processes, and drive beyond the COVID-19 era. I'm always excited to work with nonprofits because their employees are people who see the big picture very well and realize that there isn't only one path to reach your destination.

When you have everyone together—whatever format that might take—there are two specific actions that need to take place from the leadership team. The first is to figure out the best way your staff works together and how to stoke the fires of their creativity. That might take the form of everyone doing things individually, where you're asking for ideas on how to move forward in their own departments. It might look like leadership presenting some options of possible plans and discussing them in a large forum. I'm a big believer in the power of small groups, where you mix people from different departments and backgrounds and let them put their heads together to combine their strengths on the best possible answer. That's something I did internally time and again when facing new situations or something that seemed particularly daunting. I combed through my own different personas—Big City Kristoffer, Island Kristoffer, and Suburb Kristoffer—to figure out what the appropriate response was. If someone mocked my clothes on the island, I knew to not make a big deal of it because things there had the habit of escalating quickly and violently, and since I was not a native, but some kid from the States who had moved into that big, fancy house, I had very few allies.

If someone mocked my clothes in high school when I was starting to gain allies, get noticed by girls, and play sports, I could recognize it as someone being insecure about the way I was rising. They knew I could stand toe to toe with them, let them know I wasn't intimidated, and make it stop if I wanted to.

When you blend your employees' backgrounds and experiences together, that heterogeneous mix is going to really open up the possibilities because you're going to have so many people going at the problem from so many different points of view.

The third step in getting the change train underway involves a little exercise known as the Elephant on the Table. I have supreme confidence that you are all familiar with the phrase "the elephant in the room." Let's consider the Elephant on the Table to be his first cousin.

While the elephant in the room is usually thought of as something that is off-putting for a family or relationship dynamic, the Elephant on the Table deals directly with major issues in organizations that people either do not want to discuss or are unintentionally avoiding because they know the situation will be uncomfortable.

For many purposes, including our own, the Elephant on the Table is often something that forces a paradigm shift in how the organization operates. I shudder to think how many companies in different industries have avoided the Elephant on the Table for months and months as the fallout of COVID-19 eradicated their profit margins, forced them to shed payroll, and stagnated their revenue streams to unheard-of proportions. I live quite close to a popular movie theater, the kind where you sit in a plush recliner and order food off a menu and drinks from the bar while you watch the film. Their Elephant on the Table was, how do we survive when our basic business model—people sitting in close quarters to watch movies, eat, and drink—is either banned by the government or diminished to almost no demand through consumer paranoia?

For nonprofits, the Elephant on the Table is, how do we get back to the level of person-to-person connectivity that existed before COVID-19? How do we drive donations and volunteerism and passion and caring and philanthropy in an environment where in-person gatherings are limited; where hugs and handshakes are discouraged; and where there are so many people lacking basic needs from the one-two punch of the coronavirus and the resulting economic hardships that it has become difficult to frame requests for our specific causes?

It's a lot to take in, and it's unlikely your first brainstorming session is going to solve all your organization's ills in a single stroke. But getting that ball rolling is vital because the only thing worse than a bad idea is no idea at all. Organizations that assume everything is going to get back to normal or that they can just wait it out are the ones who are going to bottom out first, if they have not already! These are unprecedented times, but as we talked about previously, the COVID-19 pandemic is not the first time there has been a massive change in the world of nonprofit organizations. When change is coming or has already arrived, the worst thing to do is ignore it. The longer you allow that elephant to remain on the table, the more likely it is to send your nonprofit crashing to the ground.

Proof

Throughout this book, I'll be sharing my experiences, translating those experiences into some teachable moments, and then carrying them through a hypothetical proof of a typical nonprofit organization. This is your first encounter with that hypothetical cause. Our nonprofit is known as House of Tiny Hands[2] and it is dedicated to helping families with micro-preemies—babies born

---

2   All scenarios and names mentioned herein are purely fictional and have been created solely for training purposes. Any resemblance to existing situations, persons or fictional characters is coincidental. The information presented should not be used as the basis for any specific advice.

before 24 weeks gestation—get education on and helped with the various components necessary to ensure their tiny bundles of joy get every bit of help and every advantage possible to get them up to speed throughout their lives. A lot of parent education is involved; a lot of visits to special doctors and professionals such as nutritionists; a lot of therapists including speech, occupational, and physical are involved; and much more.

House of Tiny Hands has been operational for six years and, in 2019, it surpassed $1 million in giving for the first time in the Miami area. It is focused just on the southern tip of Florida for now, but it may expand to the rest of the state if the idea and the cause catch on. The nonprofit organization had a major gala scheduled for May 2020 at the local children's hospital, but it fell through, and with it a silent auction that had some incredibly generous donations that would have raised a ton of money. Donations have tumbled, as most people are more concerned about their own children's welfare, and Madelyn, the CEO of the organization, is getting worried about how to reinvigorate her employees, volunteers, and donors. Even if her staff can't get together in person, a Zoom or Skype call gives them all the chance to see each other's faces and connect as a group. Before doing that, she sends out an email to all her team leaders to let them know what she has in mind: a groupthink session about several key subjects that she wants to get input on. These include big-box things like how to stay interactive with current donors, how to keep publicity going in a contactless world, and how to keep volunteers engaged when 99 percent of work is being done remotely.

She encourages her team leaders to come up with a few talking points on areas in each of their departments that are being impacted by the changes going on in the big world. She doesn't want solutions yet; she doesn't want the brain trust to be pigeonholed into any one specific area before they let everyone have a voice.

Having a bit of organization with her team leaders allows Madelyn to keep the bigger meeting from running off the rails. But she doesn't want to start spitting out possible solutions without everyone in earshot because that diminishes the "we the people" approach she wants to take to the crisis at hand. Besides, she isn't foolish enough to believe that being CEO makes her the master of all great ideas. Quite the contrary; the employees who are making the phone calls, planning the events, and talking to the donors are her eyes and ears, the boots on the ground. These people have their fingers on the pulse of what people are saying and thinking. Turning away from that source of knowledge would fall somewhere between foolhardy and suicidal for the company's future.

Once her department heads are in place, Madelyn can schedule the bigger Zoom meeting, give a state of the organization address, and drive home her points on working together as a team to figure out the best course forward. She can use breakout rooms in Zoom to assign people into small groups as both an icebreaker and a refresher and pull them back into a larger roundtable location to hear the best of the best ideas.

GETTING A PLAN IN PLACE

My Story

The question of who I was going to be was one that I never had an answer to growing up. Some of it was moving around a lot, some of it was having to keep meeting new people, and some of it was that I just couldn't seem to find my niche. I would try new activities and be interested in them for a while, but then that interest would wane. That happened to me with taekwondo and judo; it happened to me with wrestling. The more I grew in the community the better things got for me, so I adapted in a way that I learned a lot about myself and decided that one day I wanted to get more involved by joining a team. Wrestling was different from any of the sports I had played in my neighborhood growing up or at my school in Haiti. I had no idea how to wrestle. It was a brand-new sport for me. It was the first organized sport I tried. Because of my size—I was so heavy compared to the average freshman—I just couldn't move as swiftly as the guys who were a lot lighter on their feet. I was only 14 years old and was a pretty solid kid, but I definitely needed a lot of coaching up. The wrestling coach, Mr. Washington, was pretty cool. He always had tons of stories to tell us, and he was a great person and an awesome character. He was also the computer science teacher at my junior high and taught me how to use a computer. His classes were always fun because I knew I was going to learn something different every time. Granted, these computers were nothing like what kids today are learning on. They were archaic in nature, MS-DOS systems with humongous screens and keyboards, but it was a great skill to have.

I didn't necessarily fit in with those kids in junior high; I had just returned from Haiti, and I didn't really know the trends. The local community school wasn't the nicest school, and it wasn't the roughest school—it was somewhere in the middle. Every day I was making a name for myself in the classroom with the teachers. I was one of the kids who would always raise my hand to participate or read something off the board. I just wasn't afraid to adapt to my surroundings. Most of the time, kids would see me in the hallway and try to recruit me to become part of their crew, but I just wasn't the person who needed to be in a group of people all the time.

When I got to my new high school, I was so tall that I gravitated toward trying out for the basketball team. My height got me on the team, there was no doubt there. Most of the other guys were way ahead of me in terms of skill level, what they could do with a basketball, and their understanding of the rules. I think some of them weren't even convinced that I could play basketball. So, I started learning the game slowly. First, I learned how to rebound. Then I learned how to pass, then how to dribble out, then how to stay in the paint. At times, my teammates started to see me making progress and they would encourage me to never quit and to always want to get involved and learn. I started to feel a sense of brotherhood when the guys on my team would lift me up during challenging moments in game situations, when the pressure was on. If I couldn't focus well enough on my own, I knew I had teammates like Shelvin, Chauncey, and Travis, who were going to be there to encourage me.

We had some real talent on the team and the coach focused on developing that talent to win as many games as possible. Some of the guys did things on the court that I'm not sure I could have done in a video game. They were able to move with the ball or without it and find angles and lanes and paths to the basket that I was not able to see. From my limited point of view, they seemed like perfect players because of the coordination they had and their connection to the game. I was a project player; I knew that, and it showed in the way I was used during games. My height could make a difference on defense, but I was limited on offense. I grew to be a good rebounder and I enjoyed that aspect of the game, but there was not a coach out there who was going to take the time to show me how to play the game of basketball.

I remember hating going to practice on Saturday morning because I was always the odd man out and I had so many things to catch up on. They considered me a raw player. I had the size, and I had the capabilities, but I just didn't have the technique or the coordination yet to manage my moves. I realized that if I really worked hard, I might continue to develop, but the team I was on was not going to be putting me on the court to accomplish that. That was a lot more difficult to understand then than it is now. I wasn't heartbroken that I wasn't playing a lot; I enjoyed the team atmosphere and being around other guys because I was always craving a sense of unity and community and I was getting some of that. But basketball wasn't my favorite sport, and with my lack of playing time, I eventually left the team.

I was still interested in physical activity and competition, so I started lifting weights with one of my friends. That was when things really started changing for me. I was always tall, but now I was putting on muscles everywhere as I got into lifting weights. My chest and my shoulders filled out and, instead of being a tall kid, suddenly I was turning into a physical specimen. People started to notice me more and more, and I started getting attention from girls, which was a first for me. I got a job working at Taco Bell and put in a ton of hours in the summertime, enough to buy my first car, which was an old police interceptor. I started driving it all over town, and people at school thought it was a real gangster car, so everyone would stop and look when it pulled up at school, and then everyone would look to see who got out of it.

I enjoyed the attention until it all came to a jarring halt. I was getting on the highway one night on my way home when I got T-boned in a huge accident. I was OK but the car wasn't, and the real problem came when it turned out I was driving without car insurance. I was 16 years old. I got a traffic ticket for causing the wreck and a bill for thousands of dollars for the damage to the cars. Needless to say, my mom and dad were furious at me, and my dad told me he was taking the car away from me for a year. A year! For a 16-year-old, you might as well tell him you're taking the car away for a century. With no cooler ride, I went back to my first plan—hitting the weight room. I threw myself into it and got bigger and stronger every week as I headed back to school.

One day I was eating lunch in the cafeteria when the head football coach came up to me and said, "Son, you look wide. Ever thought about coming out for football?" It was a really special moment for me. I had never had a head coach of any sport come up and ask me to try out. It was an inspirational moment for me. Someone wanted me. More than that, the football team wanted me. High school football is an enormous passion in Florida. For one thing, you have three of the greatest powerhouses in college football—Miami, Florida, and Florida State—spread around the school. More than 1,700 players from Florida high schools have gone on to play in the NFL. Saint Thomas Aquinas in Fort Lauderdale has had 37 graduates make the NFL; in fact, 15 of them were active during the 2020 season. So, while I might have lost my car for the year, going out for football elevated my credibility at school like nothing else. My high school was an interesting place in that it was a huge melting pot of different cultures. There were other kids who looked like me at my school, which was a far cry from life in New York City. There were other kids who had lived in another country for a while and were now in the US, just like me. And since the school was brand new, everyone was looking for their niche and learning about one another.

So, the spring of my junior year, I went out for football, and that's where I found a whole lot of unity and brotherhood that I had been looking for my whole life. I knew a little more about football than I had about basketball, but nothing when it came to the X's and O's of the game. The coaches understood that I was raw, so they put me at nose tackle on defense, which is a position where you can just run up the middle on every single play and blow things up. If you ever watch an NFL game, look for the biggest guy on defense and you'll see him right in the middle of the line opposite from where the center is. On every snap, he's going to be bulling forward into the offensive line looking to disrupt whatever the offense is trying to do. Lots of times, it takes two offensive players just to block this one guy, which means there is a mismatch somewhere else, and the defense is going to beat the offense on that play.

As spring practice moved toward summer and then my senior year, I was getting even taller and my arm span was getting really long. Nose tackle is a vital position, but it's not really a skill position. It's kind of like being a human sledgehammer or a battering ram. The more my coaches saw of me, the more they realized I wasn't that sort of player; I was a big man with a lot of athleticism. The wingspan in particular was interesting to them because long arms make a big guy ideal to play on the offensive line. So, they moved me from nose tackle on defense to right tackle on offense. Now I was part of the plan on offense to move the ball down the field and score touchdowns. I started to see the inner workings of the team and how there had to be a plan on every single play, every single quarter, every single half, every single game, or else it would all fall apart. When nobody was on the same page, we'd get our butts handed to us by teams with way less talent. When we had practiced hard and had a great plan in place, we could beat anyone. That was a real eye-opener for me. I was seeing how things and people could mesh together to make something amazing happen.

The offensive line was the next part of my plan because I was six feet five inches and 285 pounds. I started to get noticed by other teams and then by scouts. I had never played before, so nobody knew who I was. But they saw I could do something and that made them sit up and take notice. Who was this giant we've never seen before? Where did he come from? At that point, I started realizing that maybe football could be a part of my plan after graduation. I saw that I could do something special that people were interested in me for. I needed a strategy to get out of the environment I was in. The only two choices before football started getting interesting were going to college or joining the military. Staying at home was not a good idea. The kind of guys at school who didn't go to college or the military after graduation wound up being drug dealers and thugs. That's not what I wanted to be about. My mentality about the military was that I wanted to be hardcore and take the hardest route, which for me meant the Marine Corps. But suddenly I got good at football and real college scouts were paying attention. I started getting letters from all over the country. Schools wanted me to come visit or sign a letter of intent to receive a scholarship. I got letters from Oregon, Wisconsin, Rutgers, Miami, and Nebraska.

But there's where the plan almost ended in disaster. To sign a Division I scholarship, you have to have a test score—either the SAT or the ACT—in place by February 3 of your senior year. For most college football recruits, they know this process forward and backward by the time they're in high school because they have their eyes on the prize of what a scholarship means. My parents didn't know anything about how college athletics work, and I didn't either. My head coach either didn't realize what was going on or assumed my family knew how to play the game, because February 3, 2005, rolled around and I hadn't taken either test, meaning no college could offer me a scholarship to play football. So suddenly my rapid ascent through college ball was looking more and more like an unmitigated disaster.

Fortunately, I was saved at the last minute. Even though every Division I school had given out all their football scholarships by signing day, Division II schools were still active on the market. My coaches had posted game film online in an effort to show more coaches and scouts what some of my teammates and I could do. At my height and weight, I stuck out like a sore thumb in the middle of all those guys and I started getting calls from Division II schools. One of the ones who called was the University of Charleston in West Virginia. It helped enormously that their coach was from Florida, and when I mentioned I still didn't have a test score, he told me to go get one as fast as I could, and he'd make sure it was ready to go when they sent me an offer.

Teachable Moments

Any organization without a game plan is an organization destined for failure, plain and simple. It's a tough thing to break down to some of the clients I've worked for because they are absolutely amazing people. They have realized their passion in life is to help others and they are bearing full steam ahead to do so, but they're falling hopelessly into the category of working hard as opposed to working smart. They're throwing countless resources into everything they do and the only thing that's happening is their budget is being depleted while they flail about looking to make a difference.

Planning is something that really separates all sorts of entrepreneurs, whether they are just starting out or have been in the game for a while. The planners take time to research every facet of what they're trying to accomplish. They make sure they have a specific set of steps in place to take to reach their destination and fallback steps for each of those in case they don't happen to work. Those who don't plan are the kind of people who decide to go on a road trip by getting in their cars and just driving as fast as they can in one direction. Sure, it can be a fun trip, but they have no idea where they are going, what to pack, or when they might run out of gas. Without a plan, the number of things that we don't know about is overwhelming. Whether we're talking about a plan to build a nonprofit or a plan to react to change, the answer remains the same. If you are not prepared, you're going to struggle and eventually fail.

When I was a senior in high school, my plan was either to find a college that would accept me and start taking classes to figure out my next step or head for the Marines and let that choice guide my future. There were two specific paths I could take to get to the next step of my life and determine what would come next. A ton of kids in my school had zero choices going into their last year. They didn't face high school graduation saying, "What's next?" but rather, "Thank God that's over!" Nonprofits need a plan in place that is going to get them from Point A to Point B, especially in times of great change. There were so many organizations caught flat-footed by COVID-19 that they had to shut down and lay off staff; they simply had no plan in place to pivot in a new direction when finances got tight. A thing like the coronavirus and its fall-out—how could you ever plan for it? No one outside the CDC saw such a terrible event coming, and as we pass the year mark since it first started, most places are still just barely recovered. Part of our planning has to be dedicated to what we don't know, which might sound a little backwards when you first think about it: how do we plan for something when we don't know what it is? The idea is to plan for the worst, for the catastrophic, for the unexpected. At big corporations, that means planning for data breaches, hurricanes, tornadoes, and earthquakes, events where entire systems can be taken offline for long periods of time. Most nonprofit organizations don't think like that because they typically don't have to. If you're going to succeed in the long run, your game plan needs to handle all contingencies.

There's more to your game plan than what to do if a fire breaks out at the office or who you should call if you can't get into your email, however. Your plan needs to alter with the trends of society and also be able to include all opinions and perspectives in order to appeal to all people and make your organization universal. I'm talking about powerful forces like inclusion, especially when it comes to ethnicity. Your organization needs to appeal to a broad base of people in order to maximize your influence and your appeal, and one of the best ways to do that is to be composed of a broad base of people. The world has become such a melting pot that this concept needs to be embraced wholeheartedly. Including people from different walks of life and being able to collaborate with them will give you a real dynamic sense of your organization. It's important to be open-minded and ignore what people look like, how they speak, what clothes they wear, and focus on your connection to them. What kind of spirit do they have? How in touch with their emotions are there? What kind of energy do they provide to you? Energy doesn't lie about a person.

In most big corporate settings, you're finding a distinctive lack of inclusion that is only now being picked up on and exposed as social injustice. When we are able to draw from a lot of viewpoints, not only are we getting a lot more perspective on the problems we are trying to solve, but we are also exposing others that are keeping us from reaching our full potential. I've come to realize that when an organization is able to nurture being open and allowing inclusion and different perspectives from different people's views, it tends to bring an amazing new spirit of creativity. You'll start finding new ways to communicate and new ways to focus on a common goal; your mission is stronger, and your focus is narrower because you're getting the perspective of people from so many different walks of life who bring tremendous amounts of value. When you put that effort into seeing all colors and hearing as many voices as possible in your own organization, you're also going to have that strength built in the community you serve. That leads to growth and sustainability because you can really rely on that diversity on the outside looking in and vice versa.

Proof

Earlier we introduced our hypothetical nonprofit—House of Tiny Hands—dedicated to the education of and assistance for families of micro-preemie babies. Its CEO, Madelyn, is trying to figure out how to regain the momentum of the program's first six years after having to cancel its spring gala in 2020 during the COVID-19 shutdown, which ultimately forced her to furlough some of her staff and let her volunteers know that they can no longer go to the area hospitals and engage parents for the time being. Micro-preemies continue to be born all over the area, but how does her organization get that recognition through to its donors? It's time to figure out a new plan, albeit likely temporary, to get everyone moving in harmony and moving in the right direction.

When in-person events continue to be few and far between, an organization needs another way to bring people together. Zoom calls and video conferences serve their purpose, but they are still hampered by the fact that you have to be there at the time they go live to actually participate. What's lacking for Madelyn's staff, volunteers, donors, and new parents is a community that they all can get involved in on their own time at their own level of participation. That's when the lightbulb goes on in her brain. If she can't build the community in person, she can do it online, expanding the charity's website to be an interactive safe haven for all key stakeholders in the organization to come to on their own time to gain valuable information, share stories and photos, make friends with other parents going through the same shared experience, get advice, and make donations. She wouldn't need to reinvent Facebook to make it successful: she would merely need to borrow a few of its and other social media websites' best attributes; combine them with intense security to keep everyone's data safe; and advertise its existence across her charity's social media channels and with the local newspapers, TV stations, radio shows, mommy blogs, and more. She even envisioned giving parents the option of identifying themselves as being "in need" of certain things like meals, clothes, formula, etc. while they got used to life with a micro-preemie and would arrange for her donors to have the option to sponsor a specific family rather than simply giving money to a general overall fund. The sponsored family would have the option to send thank you notes back to the sponsor—even pictures or videos if they so desired—to show them that their donations were highly valued and put to good use. The charity would continue doing Zoom calls and advice videos, but they would archive them on the new site and make them available 24/7 for parents who were looking for assistance. It would not be the same as the personal touch that the charity was known for, but it would be fulfilling its mission of caring for others and making a difference, not to mention involving as many people as possible. For now, that was all that mattered.

TEAM BUILDING

My Story

It's really tough going through life alone, no matter what you're trying to accomplish. Growing up, my number of friends always seemed to be limited by where I was living, especially since we kept moving. I made a few friends in my first neighborhood in New York City, and then all of a sudden, we were moving to Florida. I was at the age then when making friends is pretty easy— everybody's outdoors playing sports, riding bikes, and getting into trouble. But that trouble was a big part of the reason that my parents up and moved us for a third time back to their home in Haiti. Talk about a culture shock! I wasn't riding my bike around the neighborhood or wandering the streets with a couple of pals from school. Our home was large and very accommodating, but it was on a big parcel of land with high fences around it to keep the trouble out. After school, I wasn't lollygagging around town seeing what kind of trouble I could get into; I knew what kind of trouble was out there, and it was the kind that left you kidnapped or dead if you got caught in the wrong part of town at the wrong time of day or night. I stayed close to home and relied pretty strictly on my own family and no one else during that time. It drew me closer to my parents and siblings, but let's just say I didn't write any letters to pen pals back in Haiti when we came back to Florida.

Back to Florida! A new school, a new city, and like 4,000 other high school kids, I was just trying to find a little niche of a place that felt like I might fit in. When you found a friend or two who enjoyed your company enough to hang out with, you held onto them tightly because it made life so much easier when someone had your back. But I got a new perspective on team building when I went out for the basketball team. I very rarely played, but I was part of a real team. We had uniforms and a locker room and fans in the stands rooting for us. The guys on the team might not have all been my best friends, but I knew when something happened on the court, every one of them had my back in the same fashion that I had theirs. Although I didn't stay on the team for long, it was an eye-opener. People of different ages and classes were drawn together by a single purpose and a single motivation.

I got an even bigger dose of it when I went out for football my junior year and then transitioned into a starter on the varsity offensive line my senior year. What a marvelous metaphor in team-building football is! An offense has 11 moving parts on every play. If even one of those parts struggles to achieve its goal, the play will break down and bad things will happen—a tackle for a loss, a sack, a turnover, a touchdown for the other team, or an injury for one of your players. Some days it felt like we couldn't even start moving on the same "hike," while other days it felt like the New England Patriots couldn't have stopped us if they tried. It was fascinating to me to see this team-building taking place. It was even more intense when I moved from defense to offense because the offensive line is its own little team within a team. Five guys—six if you're using a tight end—all having to work together in perfect harmony to make a play happen. Not just one play, but every play! Are we exploding off the ball to lose a running back between two spots on the field and see how far his speed takes him? Or are we forming a pocket around our quarterback, so he has time to select a target and fire a perfect spiral down the field? That kind of teamwork is about trust, discipline, anticipation, and learning how each other's movements and mindsets work. Being on a football team throughout high school, college, and into the professional ranks let me see what people can do when they work together for a common cause. In the best of situations, things like personal ambition and egos get pushed aside in favor of the idea that together we are so much more capable than we are apart. I carried those lessons forward past my playing days and into my professional life as a testimony to how I wanted to do business and what I wanted all of my future teams to look like.

Before I got to the pros, I started building the concept in my mind of a machine that could help offensive linemen work on their punch-and-strike technique and could be used to better their efforts in practice as well as in games. I had a great idea, but no idea how to build it—that was never my thing. I needed a handyman for the logistics who used power tools, performed measurements, and understood carpentry. So, I called up a childhood friend of mine named John who I had kept in touch with who was outstanding in those fields and told him about my ambition to build a punching board. He took right to it, as I had hoped he would. We went to the literal drawing board and as I described my idea, he sketched it out and started making a list of supplies we would need—planks, screws, a power saw, and all the other tools to bring my vision to life. We used different pads on it to give it the shape of a body. Eventually, we realized it would be a tool that two people would need to use together, where one person had the board fastened over their body and the other person would use force on it to improve their techniques. John and I had plenty of disagreements on whether this was actually going to be built, but as the process went along, we really began to work as a team. It was an eye-opener because I was from one part of the world, and he was from another. We had different fundamental ideas about how things worked and how things should look. But when we both opened our minds, we were able to collaborate based on our experiences and our upbringings. Culture was a dynamic part of how we were able to adapt and work together.

Teachable Moments

I'm not sure there is an industry outside of sports where team building is more important than it is in nonprofits. You want to create an inspired culture. Culture is the foundation and the embodiment of your organization. If the people you work with aren't passionate, inspired, dedicated, and really believe in each other, it's impossible to create a culture that is going to be successful in the nonprofit realm. An effective nonprofit culture is not just a bunch of individuals who believe in a particular cause. It's a collective understanding for all those involved, from your leadership to your staff, to your volunteers, to the community you serve. Team building is not about fun exercises where everyone gets to know each other; it is about intentionally creating a culture that is maintained by your leadership through hard work and consistency. Teams are motivated by a sense of purpose. Nobody joins a nonprofit to make a lot of money or have their ego stroked. They do it for a cause they believe in. The better the team you build, the better the culture you produce. The better the culture you produce, the more potential your nonprofit has to positively impact the community. So, what are some key factors in developing and maintaining a nonprofit culture for your team?

It starts with your entire team being on board with what your nonprofit core values are. If your leadership doesn't know what those values are, you've got bigger problems than putting the right team together. Nonprofit values should be well-established in your onboarding process and your day-to-day activities in order to line up with the actions of your leadership and staff in everything you do. One of the chief core values I like to see in place is how money is used within the organization. Another key aspect is the work-life balance that it offers its employees, as well as how it measures impact and success. Your organization's core values shouldn't just be a plaque on the wall or words on a business card, however. They should be incorporated into the organization's decision-making process to make sure everyone from the top down and the bottom up is staying committed to those values. Not everyone on the team is going to have the same opinion on every subject, but a commitment to the values that the organization holds dear is a necessity.

When you have your core values in place, you can craft a mission statement that ties them all together. A clear mission statement might attract others' attention, but it is written to inspire, motivate, and unite the team you are putting together to carry it out. It also has the unique function of reminding your team that you're serving a higher purpose. That's always one of the best ways to keep your team grounded and humble. At the end of the day, it doesn't matter how many clicks, hits, likes, or shares your post received, or even how much money you convinced a donor to contribute this year. The most paramount task for every nonprofit is to change lives for the better. Your team of staff and volunteers are not merely out working on a road construction project or trying to pitch a new soft drink to a focus group of teenagers. They have an important goal as outlined by your mission.

Culture cannot be built in a nonprofit without remarkable leadership. Your leaders should take an active role in defining your culture, especially when it comes to the overall sense of morale. During a time like the COVID-19 pandemic when people feel out of control, scared, and uncertain of the future, leadership is extraordinarily important in shaping the nature of your nonprofit's culture. It's not just about buzzwords and promises, it's about a belief system that will shape every process and purpose going forward, in good times and difficult ones.

Your organization's leadership is in charge of several key responsibilities in the nonprofit landscape, including the following:

- Determining the ways your staff works independently
- Determining the ways your staff works collaboratively
- Scheduling work hours
- Enabling work-life balance
- Determining the physical environment of the workspace
- Establishing methods of communication
- Maintaining transparency
- Distributing responsibilities

When leadership is at its best, it is open to receiving feedback as well as giving staff the opportunity to express emotions and voice opinions on achievements and failures within the team.

But leadership can do only so much. Leadership might be making the big-picture decisions, but the staff carry them out and are the most regular engagers of the community. The way you treat your staff is of vital importance to ensure that your organizational culture doesn't just look good, it allows your staff to thrive.

No one likes a toxic workplace, and the more confident your staff feel about how they are being treated, the more they will care about the success of your nonprofit. You need to ensure that your staff feel valued in their place in the organization; not that they are so many moving cogs in a machine that can be replaced if necessary. Part of this is making sure they're clear on the organization's policies across the board and have detailed knowledge of how the company's internal communications work so they can be confident in how to address issues and questions with management should the need arise. I recall a friend in another line of work giving a speech once on the most important part of customer service in his industry. Most people thought he would say communication or transparency, but his answer, and your answer, should be that his own staff carried the most weight. Their successes will ultimately lead to a better work performance and a higher level of commitment for your nonprofit. This is achieved by policies, acts, and everyday leadership that demonstrates that your staff's professional and personal growth, along with their happiness in the workplace, is of paramount importance. If your employees live in a state of fear or anxiety that failure to achieve your mission will be met with harsh or negative consequences, they will struggle to be creative and take the innovative risks required to make a nonprofit succeed, particularly in unprecedented times such as the COVID-19 pandemic.

Of course, achieving that workplace culture is a real task, much more challenging than mere words on a sheet of paper. It won't just happen overnight. The successful culture requires finding what all members of your nonprofit want, then taking charge to ensure that the interest of those involved with the organization is met. When people come to their workplace feeling that they are working toward a goal that they believe in, you're going to see them get motivated to do their best work. This starts at the top level. Encourage your staff to take risks. Treat honest mistakes with compassion and find ways to turn failures into positive learning experiences. Ensure that there is an outlet in your infrastructure where staff can generate and receive continuous, open feedback about your organization and make sure the street runs both ways. If your team feels heard, this will empower them with the knowledge that they are not merely a member of the ship's crew; they also have a hand in plotting its course. One of the most exciting elements in any journey is the freedom to choose. Give your employees the opportunity to answer these questions. What's most important to you in your career, and what activities give you the best use of your time? In answering these, an employee is taking responsibility for their own success and happiness professionally.

You might be part of the leadership team of your nonprofit, but you also work there, and you must be part of the team-building process that harnesses your own goals if you want to succeed in your mission. It's therefore important that you periodically revisit your own main goals to ensure that you're still on the path that you desire. I can't tell you how many people I've encountered over the years who have recently been promoted to a leadership position only to realize that it's taken them away from the thing they love best—whether that's engaging directly with their targeted community; being the person on the phones selling people on the value of a charitable donation; or going out in the field doing the physical work of building houses, digging wells, helping people kick bad habits, etc. The good news is that the social impact sector is more vibrant and varied than ever. Whether you are struggling in management or feel like your talents could be used in an expanded role greater than what you're doing as a staff member, the opportunities exist for you to do so. This is another positive of working for an organization that has a great open communication policy; you can make time to talk to your unit leader or the head honcho and let them know what you're feeling, where you're at, and what sort of future you'd like to see for yourself. Most nonprofit employees resemble Swiss Army knives to begin with: taking on multiple functions with a significant skill set that allows them to pivot from one to the next over the course of a day. The last thing you want for yourself is to get mired in a position that isn't fulfilling your personal desires in a professional environment. When nonprofit work becomes an unpleasant grind, your passion will get chipped away and damaged, and you won't be capable of doing your best work any longer. Within a well-oiled organization, there should be room for you to try new things, whether it's shadowing another position a couple of times a week or blending your responsibilities to where you can be both an internal administrator and an outreach team member who still regularly connects to the community. Flexibility has always been one of the great standard-bearers when it comes to nonprofit success, and that should extend inside your own organization if you are starting to feel more and more like the square peg in the round hole. When you review your current situation, set your goals up to what you would like to be doing, and approach someone in the organization who has the power to help you. Keep in mind that your goals should follow the SMAART mindset—that is, they should be specific, measurable, ambitious, attainable, relevant, and time-based. You could keep them quantifiable by counting backwards through time on what your goals look like. Write down what you want to be doing in 10 years' time, then 5 years' time, then a year from now. This allows you to break up your long-term career goals into short-term goals, which can go a long way toward preventing you from getting overwhelmed or discouraged.

Proof

Over at House of Tiny Hands, Madelyn is pleased with how her plan to develop an interactive community portal is coming together. She floated the idea at a staff meeting, realizing that this was going to be a major shift in the way the organization operated, so she ensured that there was structure in place to get everyone on board with the idea before cementing the plan. This included a two-pronged method. First was a question-and-answer session about the site with the whole staff on a Zoom call, including an impromptu brainstorming session on what the portal's functionality should include. She got some amazing responses in this session and believes they will go a long way in helping to shape what the product ultimately looks like. But Madelyn knows people and she knows about meeting dynamics, especially those in an imperfect environment like a video conferencing call. No matter how passionate of a staff she has—and they definitely are—you're mixing a whole lot of personality types in an unusual social setting when you turn a standard Zoom call into a rapid-fire idea generation session. Your Type A personalities are going to see it as their time to shine with great ideas and potentially some career-building maneuvering as well, eager to impress leadership with their originality. Meanwhile, the staff members who do their best work quietly and independently are going to be passive in such a dynamic, either too shy to speak up or too focused on getting through this meeting and back to their best work environment—peace and quiet!

This is one of the reasons that Madelyn makes the announcement a two-pronged approach. She wants input from everyone, not only because they are all part of the team, but because of their rich diversity as an amazing melting pot of different experiences and cultures that they bring to the organization. About an hour after the Zoom call ends, they'll all get an email from her thanking them for all their hard work during the pandemic and asking for their further help in making the new portal a success. The email will include a form for them to fill out asking them a series of pointed questions about their opinions and ideas for how the portal can best serve the community. While some organizations shy away from making a point of a person's gender, race, or sexual persuasion, CEO Madelyn's questions will celebrate those differences and tell her employees point-blank that their personal knowledge in what makes them unique is vital to the project's success and the nonprofit's ability to keep fulfilling its mission statement during the current events of the world.

She'll charge her employees to help her identify how each sub-set population of the community they serve can best be engaged. What will help them trust that the portal is there to help them, not merely collect their information? What existing social media websites are they the most comfortable using and why? If they have limited Internet access, where can they go to use it reliably? What would be their biggest areas of interest in such an environment: Watching videos? Reading articles? Engaging with other parents of micro-preemies? Sharing photographs? She also wants to pick their brains on her idea of pairing parents in need with donors who want that personal touch of sponsoring a family. How will different types of families respond to this idea? Will they embrace the help or be offended that they are being asked to take a handout? Will they be interested in potentially communicating with the donor or sharing family photos, or will they see such requests as invasions of their privacy? She's not expecting her staff to have all the answers, but she is hopeful that they can provide her enough insight to make the best decisions that will move the company successfully forward.

It's not just a one-and-done approach for Madelyn. She wants her employees' ideas, but she wants to hear them in their own voices. The form is more of a documentation exercise to get their words out of their heads while the idea is still fresh. When they return the form to her, they'll get an invite for an in-person or Zoom follow-up session, one-on-one with her, to discuss their ideas. She feels that those who struggle in a large group environment will do better in a more intimate format where they don't have to worry about who will say what to their ideas and they can speak openly and honestly with her. She assures them that this has nothing to do with anyone's job performance and there are no bad ideas, except for the ones that aren't brought to light. Not only does this give her more insight into her new project, but it also builds the bond of trust between the CEO and her staff. If employees see the head honcho as someone who is unapproachable or who doesn't have time to talk to them, the gap between leadership and staff grows, and with the slightest of pushes can turn into an unpleasant "us" vs. "them" mentality that threatens to undo any team building or culture building that you have put in the work for. It is difficult for most CEOs to have a true "open-door" policy, but at the very least, a system that enables employees to schedule time for a chat is both reasonable and easily done with today's technology.

When Madelyn goes through her one-on-one meetings and calls, she makes sure to do a lot more listening than talking so that she is giving her employees the floor and so that they recognize that their voices are being heard; this is not a session for the boss to wax poetic on her hopes and dreams for the organization, but for each staff member to make the new idea their own and share their vision of it. She'll then ask them if they would like the extra responsibility of being a caretaker of the portal, getting user permissions to moderate it, and explain what that implies: ensuring that every member of the online community is being respected by and respectful toward everyone else. This request is an opportunity for her staff to take on extra duties and showcase their own abilities. Remember that discussion about how her Type A personalities all probably spoke out in the meeting while the Type Bs were quiet and aloof? A lot of Type B personalities can be a lot more comfortable in the digital environment than in the physical one. By asking them to take on a moderator role on the organizations' new portal, she might be giving them the chance to shine in a more assertive role in an ecosystem they feel more comfortable in. Madelyn will also ensure that there is a place where employees can give feedback and constructive criticism about the portal. If they see red flags or have concerns, she wants them brought directly to her attention; there's no chain of command in place here, but a direct line to the top. This reinforces her connection to her staff and how much she values what they have to say. If someone spots an issue, they have the knowledge that the email they send isn't going to sit in a receptionist or assistant's inbox for three days; it will make its way straight to Madelyn within the next business day.

This is just one small sliver of how Madelyn builds her organization's team and promotes the culture of success. She has to acknowledge that for some people, the portal is not nearly as important as the actual work in the community, and she needs to find ways to keep those employees engaged and active. The internet might be the most transcendent invention of the last one hundred years, but not everyone lives there. Madelyn must find ways to engage her less technology-inclined employees as well and ensure that they are having their professional needs met to get the best work and commitment out of them. What does this look like? It depends on their particular strengths and skillsets. For some, it might be in writing new copy for the nonprofit's mailer campaigns and signage around town. For others, it can be continuing to engage its donor list in traditional methods like phone calls. While just about everyone in a non-blue-collar job is using the internet in some capacity during their day-to-day, Madelyn wants to ensure that those who are less comfortable with it among her staff, and particularly her volunteers, are able to feel they are making a difference regardless.

Speaking of that new portal, it needs a name and an unveiling at some point. She wants to get the best ideas for both, so she reaches out to her entire staff, plus the volunteers, and asks for ideas. She further incentivizes it by offering those who come up with the top choices being gift cards to their favorite restaurant and a few other perks. This is another great way to build culture. Staff is not just being asked to do tasks because they are the employees, they are being incentivized with rewards that give them a sense of satisfaction and further their work-life balance. Madelyn has all submissions reviewed by her fellow members of the leadership team and then has three to five finalists given out to the entire staff and the nonprofit's social media followers in a vote. The winner is the simple yet elegant "Portal 2 Hope," a name that signifies the most powerful weapon that the parents of micro-preemies have in those first frightening days—hope. One of her non-internet users is a talented artist who prefers paper to pixels. She designs a banner for the big unveiling—which is done virtually—but in a format that lets media members and internet users be part of the festivities. The catchphrase "Unmasking Our Potential" is generated to celebrate the portal's debut, with the clever double meaning of the organization looking forward to a future where COVID-19 and facemasks are fading into our distant memory.

CHAPTER 3

Standing Out in Your Community

While 99 percent of nonprofits are out there with incredible causes, standing up for the little guy, promoting awareness, and trying to deliver messages of hope and peace, it's still very much a competition.

You're competing with other causes for time and attention. You're competing for dollars inside a donor's pocketbook against their basic needs, their other charitable donations, and their own impulse purchases and dreams. You're also competing against malaise and boredom. When people see you having the same blood drive or bake sale year after year to raise funds or push donations, what's inspiring them to continue to care?

Just like in every other industry on Earth, you must stand out and get noticed to be a success. Good intentions are not enough, sad to say. You might be the most passionate person who has ever lived when it comes to your cause, but if you can't get people's attention, hold it, and turn it into positive results, you're going to face a long uphill slog that is going to more likely end in bankruptcy than a spot on the local news. You have to stand out, and in the digital age, that brings with it both good news and bad news. The bad? It's more challenging because everyone has access to the same tools of promotion. The good? Very few people know how to use them that well. How do you stand out? How do you perpetuate that momentum? You have to think creatively; you have to take carefully considered risks, strategize, and adapt. Let's start our deep dive into this crucial component of nonprofits by taking a look back into my formative years.

STANDING OUT IN YOUR COMMUNITY

My Story

Despite some of my natural shyness, as well as the fact that I always felt like the new kid at school and that most people couldn't figure out what race or nationality I was, I tended to stand out wherever I went. Being the tallest kid at school can have that effect on you. I was six feet, five inches by my senior year of high school, and topped out at six feet, seven inches in college. More than a few times in secondary school I got mistaken for a parent or a teacher or a coach while roaming the hallways. I always found this hilarious. Still, with two years of school left to go, my height was about the only thing that people noticed me for. That was disappointing for me. I was smart, I wanted girls to notice me, and like any typical teenager, I craved the attention that I couldn't seem to generate. That year I decided to get committed to improving the way my body looked.

I decided to get into the weight room and get more serious about weight training. I had a buddy named Jose, another tall guy like me who wasn't the most muscular cat in school, and we started working out together every day after school. Making that commitment with another person was the incentive we both needed to make it happen in the weight room. I started realizing my potential beyond just being a tall guy who was big enough that nobody would mess with, but not standing out enough for people to take a second look. As I put in day after day of training, I found my shoulders getting stronger and my chest starting to look firmer. I was about six feet, three inches tall and 205 pounds when I started, and Jose and I were always partnering up to hit the bench press and break our own records. It was great having somebody there to count your reps, relive funny things that had happened at school, and just talk about what was going on in our lives. We counted on each other. Before I found my true calling on the football team, Jose and I were a team of two.

As my body started to develop, I felt like I was walking taller and feeling more confident. My school shirts were filling out more and the hot girls in gym class were noticing me more and more. The coaches of other sports started to sniff around too, so I knew I was on the right path to get their attention away from who was already on the field. I had never been that serious about playing any sport; it was mostly just the idea of finding something to be a part of for me.

As I related in an earlier chapter, one day the school's head football coach, Coach Rogers, walked right up to me at lunch and asked if I was interested in playing football. I had no response because it was the first time a coach came to me and was genuinely interested. I watched football on TV, but I knew very little about how to play it or how a team really worked. But I knew I was bigger than every other guy at school and that I might be able to not only help the football team succeed but open a door for myself to an opportunity to go to college. My parents knew very little about organized sports. The only thing they understood was what was played in the community—loosely organized neighborhood activities. Coach Rogers painted a far different picture for me. He talked about how everybody watched the athletes on the field—meaning my fellow students, parents, and scouts from colleges. If I was good enough, I might find myself being offered a scholarship to play in college and attend free of charge.

I made the decision to stand out. I was already getting attention for my size, but I wanted to do more than that. It was my last couple of years of high school, and I wanted them to be memorable. Coach Rogers really motivated me with the picture he painted of what could be. He talked to me very simply, not like a teacher talking down to a kid, but like a man recognizing that I had ability and potential and trying to help me realize it. He set me up to succeed by not putting any initial pressure on me; he just invited me to come out to practice, check it out, and see if it might be something that I'd like to do. That sort of approach really stayed with me. If you've ever played organized sports, I bet you have had a coach who is a yeller and a screamer and makes you feel worthless whenever you make any kind of mistake. On the flip side, I hope you've also had a coach who makes you feel like you have the chance to be part of something special and that you're having an opportunity presented to you. Coach Rogers was the latter for me.

This will probably sound funny in retrospect, but I had no idea what position I might play when I got out to my first practice. I thought having my hands on the ball looked good, maybe I could be the guy who throws it? Fortunately, for my own future and that of my teammates and coaches, my high school already had a quarterback and didn't need the six-foot-three, 250-pound Haitian to take over under center. They put me on the defensive line instead, and once I was there, my opening mindset was that I was taller than everyone else, I had a wider arm span, and I could just push guys out of the way until I got to the quarterback or the guy with the ball and tackle them to the ground.

Of course, if that was all it took, everyone would be an All-Pro defensive end like J.J. Watt or Khalil Mack. I had no idea that being a great defensive end was really more about things like speed off the edge; developing spin moves and swim moves to confuse an offensive lineman; and being mentally prepared to anticipate if the offense was going to call a pass, which meant you did your thing, or a run, which meant you had to play it smart and not race past the guy with the ball. Just being on the field was not enough to be great, you had to work harder, get smarter, and use all your resources to be great. I figured I could just mimic the guys in front of me and learn the position. I didn't know the football lingo, and everything seemed to be moving way too fast for me. The coaches saw it too, fortunately, and switched me from defensive end to defensive tackle.

Instead of being on the edge of the formation, trying to race past an offensive tackle to get to the quarterback before he could release the ball, now I was in the middle of the line, going toe-to-toe against offensive guards and the center. I was now focused on strength and power rather than speed and quickness. I might still get in the quarterback's face and put him on his butt, but my main job was disruption. Deny the offense the holes it was trying to create for its running back. Get my hands in the air to limit the quarterback's field of vision. Collapse the pocket to make him uncomfortable and force him to throw on the run, drastically reducing the likelihood of him hitting his intended target for a positive gain.

The more reps I got on the defensive line, the more confident I was there. I've always been stronger in the arms than other kids my age—even when I wasn't doing any weight training at all. I was able to leverage my height, my weight, and my wingspan. I call it the Haitian strength gene. The coaches started to notice it too, particularly when we would do a drill at practice to see who the hardest hitter on the team was. It was a team-building exercise that got everyone hyped and really let us get all that energy out. The entire team would circle up on the field and start chanting like we were celebrating victory; everyone was into it. At that moment, all the cliques and the smaller groups of friends based on race, status, or even classification vanished. It felt like the most humongous football game in the world, but there were no fans in the stands; no one was watching but the players and the coaches. A guy would jump into the center of the circle and wait for another guy to do likewise. It was a hit drill where you would go one-on-one with another player, pure smash-mouth football, to see who the better hitter was.

So, a linebacker named Antonio who had played for a long time jumped out to challenge me. Coach Rogers never said as much, but I think he knew that I didn't know what I was doing and wanted to not only make an example out of the big guy, but show the other guys that size isn't the number one thing on the field; your work ethic, drive, and will win make a huge difference. You start off ten yards apart in the challenge and when the whistle blows, you go straight at each other and see who puts who on the turf. I was standing six feet, five inches by then, easily the tallest guy on the team, but I had no idea that the true secret in a one-on-one scenario like that was to get low and use your center of gravity to take out the other player. Antonio was shorter than me and came charging at me. He lowered his helmet and drilled it and his shoulder pads right into my belly. It was the hardest I had ever been hit by another person and the first time my stomach had absorbed a blow like that. I felt like my skeleton had jumped out of my body based on the shockwaves I felt. Luckily for me, that Haitian strength allowed me to absorb the hit, but I was still staggered by the blow. I realized at that moment that football was a game of inches, and this was a game where the lowest man wins.

It was my second wake-up call when it came to football and athletics. It also made me realize that on the football field, you never know what to expect. But as long as you're prepared and you're in a good position, there's always a better outcome for whatever challenge you face as the season progresses. So, I made a point to learn as much as I could about every aspect of my position. I started having some good reps at defensive tackle in practice and then started playing pretty well in scrimmages too. I was picking up nuances of the individual plays, not just doing the same actions over and over again. I started to build confidence and my coaches started realizing I could be a real X factor on the team—something our opponents didn't see coming and wouldn't know how to deal with. As the drills got more and more simple, I started seeing stepping-stones that were going to take me off the practice field and onto the playing field.

I'll never forget the first time that happened in a game against Varela Senior High. The coaches put me in at nose tackle, which means I lined up directly across from the center—the guy hiking the ball. Varela had a tall quarterback, which always helps signal-callers see the field better, but their interior line—the guards and center—were weak and disorganized. When the center hiked the ball, I blasted out of my stance and drove right through that center to drill the quarterback for a sack! The crowd cheered and all my teammates were excited. The coaches screamed their approval.

The feeling that I had when I turned around and saw and heard all of that was through the roof. It was the best thing, the most amazing feeling. We won the game and suddenly there was film of me, Kristoffer Doura, a high school football player, blowing up an offensive line and recording his first career sack. I started playing more and more and it was a good position, somewhere that my size and my work ethic allowed me to be a difference-maker.

One day the coaches came to me and said they wanted to talk; I had no idea what was going on. They confided in me that our offensive line was in bad shape and the weaknesses there were keeping us from having a shot to win a lot of games because we could never move the ball consistently enough to score points. They wanted me to switch from playing defensive line to offensive line. There was some natural inner resistance on my part, of course; who wouldn't feel that way? I was really getting good as a defensive tackle and now they want me to move to the other side of the ball, giving up my honed abilities to disrupt backfields and make tackles for a loss and sacks. But I went along with the switch because I wanted to do right by my teammates and coaches.

They moved me to right tackle, which meant I was matching up against the same defensive ends who had been ahead of me when I first came to practice. The coaches talked about things like kick slides and pass protection, and I didn't know what those things meant yet. I had to understand the role of the position before I could get into technique. However, as that awareness came, it began to dawn on me that my body type was actually a really good fit for playing offensive line. Being a right tackle meant I played to the far right of the quarterback on the edge. Being right-handed meant that the majority of my power was on the right side of my body. When those defensive ends would try to bull past me on the edge to get to the quarterback, they ran right into my strength, and it was lights out.

With my arm length and strength, I became a natural on the offensive line. I could extend my wingspan and keep defenders from getting past me. I was still one of our better defenders, so I wound up playing on both sides of the ball throughout the season. Surprisingly though, I began to enjoy the offensive line position and really favored it over defense, something I would have scoffed loud and long at even a month before. I started getting noticed just by my classmates (especially the girls, thank you very much) and teammates, but also by coaches from other teams and by scouts. As I said earlier in this book, Florida in general, and South Florida in particular, are hotbeds for college football talent. Invariably, scouts would be coming to our games throughout the year to look at some player they had been following for a few seasons and wind up noticing me in addition, asking my coaches, "Where did this guy come from?"

As a result, I started getting letters in the mail from universities asking if I was interested in playing football at the next level. They weren't just from the local junior college either. My senior year of football was the autumn of 2004. Barry Alvarez from Wisconsin sent a letter. His Badgers went 9–3 that fall and sent seven guys to the NFL draft the next April. Oregon sent one from way up in the Pacific Northwest, and who wouldn't want to play for the team that Nike's CEO supported? Auburn offered the pageantry and history of the SEC, not to mention playing a Tiger team that had gone 13–0 the year before and wound up ranking number two in the nation. There was Nebraska, which had produced literally hundreds of NFL players, including nine winners of the Outland Trophy for best lineman in the country. And the golden goose had made contact—Miami University. If you were a male child living in southern Florida and didn't dream of playing football one day for the Miami Hurricanes, most people thought there was something wrong with you. A nine-win season was considered a down year for the Hurricanes at the time I was going to high school. They weren't just the best athletes in Florida, they turned into the best players in the NFL. Michael Irvin went there. Ray Lewis. Ed Reed. Warren Sapp. Andre Johnson. Edgerrin James. Devin Hester. Jim Kelly. Jerome Brown. Cortez Kennedy. I could go on, but this book is not meant to be a million words long!

The point is that my natural abilities, my work ethic, and my desire to get better now had me standing out among the best players not only in my own district, not only in my own city, not only in the state of Florida, but across the country as well. I even started mastering the kick-slide, which is a tactic to slow down those very speedy defensive ends that would like to line up in a wide alignment to create an angle past me. The kick-slide would let me leverage the weight on my inside foot to make the defensive end get around a long corner to get to the quarterback. That makes him have to go deeper up field before he can engage with the tackle and allows me to step laterally and a little bit backwards, my shoulders square with the line of scrimmage, to engage him with my hands and arms. For all my size and strength, learning these specific tactics really made me gain a new understanding for the sport. More to the point, it was a game of positioning, and being able to fill the slot I needed on the field was critical to our offense gaining yards and scoring points. While past protection was a big deal, I also had holes to fill to generate gaps for our running backs to squeeze through and get up field. The more I understood, the more dangerous I became for opposing defenses to contend with. The more dangerous I was, the more I could be a force for change on my own team.

By the time I was starting in college and thinking about what the NFL might have to offer for me, I had grown to six feet, seven inches and weighed in at 340 pounds. Now you might expect a man of that size to move with the speed of a glacier, but you'd be mistaken. I was one of the fastest guys on the team and I had great footwork. My body fat index was just 16 percent, meaning I wasn't hunched over on the line carrying a lot of weight in my chest; I was standing tall and scanning the field on every play. Every day when we went through our opening drills to get into the groove to play the game, we would start with a punch drill. Now, this isn't the kind of punch you throw in a barroom brawl, this is the punch that an offensive lineman uses when the ball is hiked and he snaps his arms up into a pass-block stance, driving his hands and arms forward into his opponent's body. Most times, linemen practice doing this against a tackling dummy, but that first drill of the day was man on man, and I had the strongest punch on the offensive line. My punches were lethal, and when I punched a guy, he could feel it in his heart. Sometimes guys would get hurt going against me in those drills because I took them deadly seriously, and they were just going through the motions. For me, those drills were the chance to learn more about where my hands were and how my footwork was progressing. The more I could build my technique in practice, the more fluid I would be in the motion of the game. Some of my biggest challenges were in the preparation even before practice began, when I would be pushing to get the right techniques down and be able to really demonstrate my ability on those repetition drills. When you practice the right way, you start building anticipation of what you can accomplish when you get on the field for real. I learned a lot of drills and I learned a lot about how to properly position my body and become a lot stronger as an offensive lineman. I was able to translate those drills off the field into real-life situations, knowing that practice really does make perfect, and practice really builds the excitement inside of you to do well.

Doing drills provided me with the foundation of being able to build the right routine as an offensive lineman. You start to harness the anticipation of knowing that no matter what is coming your way, you're going to have a solution for it. If my opponent strikes me with a special move, a hammer hook, or a fast pass rush that I haven't seen before, it really goes back to practice in my drills. I use this as an analogy to demonstrate how nonprofit organizations are able to continue to react to adversity and change and come out on top. We'll explore that more in the next section, but it's not just about making a splash with events and fundraisers and celebrity appearances. It's about the day-to-day management of your organization and how such an operation requires practice and patience so that when it's game time, you have created the environment to have a smooth experience.

Teachable Moments

Remember how I said in the opening of this chapter that it's a lot tougher to stand out in your community these days because everyone has access to the same tools? It's what tools you use, how you use them, and how you put to work your God-given abilities that really allow you to establish your own niche and rise above the rest when you're running a nonprofit.

No matter where you are operating out of, there are going to be similar nonprofits with the same mission out there that are your competitors, whether you like it or not. Giving and supporting are acts we can all champion, regardless of who is performing them. However, if you had felt that the nonprofits already in operation were doing a perfect job, you never would have started yours in the first place. There is no doubt that you got into the nonprofit industry because you believe that there is something special in you that can make a difference. That's a great feeling and is an absolute necessity for find your spot in all the chaos out there.

Standing out in your community first and foremost means getting to know your community and making sure they know you back. This starts at the root level, the boots on the ground level as the military calls it. You have to get the awareness of yourself, your organization, and its cause out there for people to start giving you their time and attention. People don't give to the Salvation Army every Christmas because they are impressed by a person with a Santa hat outside the Home Depot ringing a bell. They give because they know the organization's history, they understand what it's raising money for, and they're proud to donate their part. What does your organization stand for? How do you let the community know that you're invested in its future success?

A great way to start is by engaging at the school level. Sponsor events. Sponsor a giveaway. Give every kid at the Friday-night basketball game a free T-shirt with your organization's logo on the front and a mission statement on the back. Call the principal's office at the local high school and tell them you're looking for volunteers for a great cause and offer to call it an internship that students can put on their college applications. Sponsor a float in the town's homecoming parade. Print out bumper stickers for a local sports team that has won a district title and let everyone know they can get one for free by stopping by your office.

The first step is getting seen and recognized as a force for good in the community and as an organization interested in promoting the good things that community is accomplishing. Host events where you partner with well-known businesses, local leaders, or local celebrities to endorse and play off their success and recognition. Invite the local newspaper or TV station to come out and cover it. You're giving them an easy win for the next edition of the nightly broadcast and you're giving yourself a talking piece about your organization that will promote it past your own borders.

The mission is what drives nonprofits but getting new donors and young people involved is what is going to perpetuate it into the future. How do young people and young donors communicate? They use text messages and emails and social media. You need to do the same thing. You need marketing campaigns that engage your potential donors on multiple channels and find out the best way to communicate with them where they are most likely to respond back. Use the power of Facebook, Twitter, Tik-Tok, and Instagram—all totally free—to engage people who are showing interest in your organization. Publish fascinating, shareable statistics on your Twitter and encourage people to retweet them to their followers. Encourage Instagram followers to hashtag your organization when they post something relevant. Collect email addresses through free giveaways and information drops to build your own mailing list. Constantly be building a database of potential donors, volunteers, and business partners.

Proof

House of Tiny Hands doesn't have a problem with getting repeat donations. Once Madelyn or one of her staff members has someone's attention, it's hard to resist getting out the checkbook—particularly when pictures of premature babies a few days old are presented next to updated photos once they've filled out, opened their eyes, and begun exploring their environments. The tough part is getting to that point. Helping out struggling infants and their brave families isn't the tough part; that comes from competing against the hundreds of other charities in Miami and the entire state of Florida for potential donors' time, attention, and interest. Between childhood diseases, hunger funds, education charities, helping kids who have lost one or both parents, all the good causes for disabilities, and other social welfare needs, it's like 500 kids showing up at the same house on Halloween to say, "Trick or treat!" No matter how generous the homeowners are, there's only so much candy in the dish.

That means CEO Madelyn has to pick her battles, do her homework, and identify population segments that are much more likely to lend a hand. She finds that there are huge communities of parents of premature babies on the internet, specifically Facebook. These parents, predominantly mothers, have formed a tight-knit community of those who have had success stories and those who have had tragedies. She finds that they range in age from their early 20s up into senior citizens, who had their own stories decades earlier and are grateful to have a discussion group full of people who know their grief and joy.

Madelyn is wise enough to know she can't simply come crashing into the discussion groups asking for money. Nothing turns a population off faster than a newcomer who is looking to take without even a hint of giving first. So, she joins the group with utter transparency as her main objective, telling her own story of being a premature twin and the many trials she underwent to even leave the hospital, much less begin living a normal life. Instead of asking for donations, she asks for knowledge—specifically, what these parents would have wanted most as a resource when they realized they were going to have a premature baby and that, instead of 24 hours at the hospital, their children might be spending weeks or months there, with limited time to be held or fed by their parents. The fact that she was a micro-preemie herself has great value in these close-knit circles, and the moms slowly open up to her through message board posts and emails. She doesn't turn down anyone's idea—if it was enough for at least one person to want it, it stands to reason that someone else might as well.

Over time, she realizes how many powerful untold stories there are in the group, and she asks permission to use them to construct a book—stories of hope for new parents of micro-preemies. She promises them anonymity if they want it or the freedom to use their real names, and a copy of the book when it comes out. The proceeds will go directly into the charity to be turned around for good use. She also plans to give away free copies to anyone making a donation above a certain dollar amount.

The idea is a smash because Madelyn has found a way to not only involve the community but involve a segment of it that might otherwise never have their stories told—mothers of premature babies are utterly devoted to making those tiny bundles of joy. Many of the mothers are justifiably proud of telling their stories in print and make sure to spread the word of the book and the charity through their own social circles. This allows Madelyn to interface with other women with similar experiences and continue picking their brains. It's a vital step because mothers who currently have micro-preemies often find the day-to-day, minute-to-minute experience so overwhelming that it's tough to put their specific needs into words. Those with the gift of hindsight are much better at vocalizing what could have gone more smoothly.

When the book is released, Madelyn contacts every news agency in the city—magazines, newspapers, well-positioned blogs and podcasts, TV, and radio stations. She pitches it as representation for a significantly underrepresented but heroic set of women whose stories have never been told before. When she gets a bite on someone wanting to do a story, she contacts some of the women who wrote their stories and convinces them to come with her and tell their stories firsthand. Doing so keeps the focus on the cause, not the charity, but the organic buzz it creates is priceless.

When word spreads about the struggle of having a micro-preemie during the pandemic, Madelyn reaches out to local businesses—hotels, restaurants, and the like—to see if they are interested in partnering with her charity to provide NICU parents with basic needs services like hot meals they can have delivered to the hospital and free or discounted rooms at hotels near the hospital their children are staying in so they don't have to make long commutes every morning and night to visit their babies. It's an easy win for the businesses, who have their own public relations departments and thus can churn out all sorts of copy promoting their collaboration with House of Tiny Hands. Now the charity is getting press in other states and cities, and demand for the book is necessitating a second printing. People might be split across political lines and racial tensions, but everyone can agree that a baby weighing two pounds at birth is worth fighting for.

HEARTBEAT

My Story

If you watch a lot of sports on TV or in person, you might assume that every athlete's heart is racing a mile a minute while they're on the field, the court, or the diamond. From the outside looking in, it would make sense. You're about to take off running at a moment's notice—racing to first base, boxing out for a rebound, or making a pancake block to free a running back and make a big gain. It's not really the case, however. Sure, your heart is pounding extra when you're doing work—running for a long touchdown, chasing down a line drive in the gap, or taking an outlet pass and going coast to coast for a dunk. But if you know what you're doing and have prepared for the moment, your pulse is going to be steady and your heart beating at a calm, even pace up until the moment you need to act. It's only when an athlete is unprepared does his fear and anxiety spike up and his heart rate begin to rise. Those are signs that he hasn't analyzed the situation well enough to have a good gauge of what's coming next. When your whole job performance relies on how well you can predict what is coming next and get yourself in a position to stop it, a lack of knowledge makes for a very difficult problem.

Think about your own line of work. When you're on a deadline and things aren't going well, you will naturally get stressed. You will sweat; you will nervously drum your fingers; you will get distracted more easily; and you are more prone to making mistakes. Not surprisingly, your pulse will be pounding in your chest. Now compare that to the feeling of working on a project that you enjoy, that you have a lot of passion for, and that you understand easily. The work will come naturally because you've got a knack for it. You'll move through it smoothly and easily because it feels like an extension of you. There's no need for your heart to pump extra blood to your thinking centers or your extremities because you aren't in a flight-or-fight response.

When I was first playing football in high school, my heart was racing on every play because I didn't have enough experience to know what to do next. I had my bread-and-butter skills, but they were only going to work on some opponents, not each and every one. I needed to find the combination of raw skills, intellect, film study, and flat-out instincts to figure out what was coming and how I could stop it. At first, this happened basically never. Then a few times a game I would guess right and be really happy and do exactly what needed to be done to turn the play into a success. As

I got into college, this started to be the case the majority of the time. Instead of guessing the right combination of things to do on each snap, I began to make the right choices beat by beat—and my heartbeat was staying the same as I went through the permutations of every play: bulling ahead to open holes for a tailback, dropping back to secure the pocket for the quarterback, deking a defensive lineman into thinking he had me beat while we were really setting up a screen pass, and so on. I was developing consistency, and it was becoming evident in those around me. I wasn't just the tall guy with the muscular arms that couldn't block a sixth grader during my first few practices. I was becoming consistent in the things I was doing. When our offense switched formations from a run-heavy look to a spread set, I was no longer being shuttled to the sideline to be subbed out, I was a part of the solution for every formation.

When I was able to stay on the field consistently and combined my effort with my talent and my growing maturity, the rhythm I was playing with started to change again. Now I was the one setting the beat on the line. My play was dictating more and more where the weakness in the defense would be. The other team knew they had to plan for me, but even then, it was usually a failed effort. In the huddle, I was giving our quarterback and running backs the confidence, they needed that I was going to be there for them and give them the time or the space they needed to get their jobs done.

When you get to that point, you can see other people start to gravitate toward you. They have noticed you leading by example and now you're giving them the vocal leadership that makes them appreciate you even more. When you reach that level of respect from those around you, that's when you're able to start making changes that really matter. On the offensive line, it was a commitment inside a commitment. It was the belief that five guys operating as one unit could do things that would dictate the course of a drive, a quarter, a half, a game, and a season. That was the progress I made from that first day, stepping onto the field in high school just trying to make sure I had my helmet secured the right way and my pads in the right places, to the end of my career, when I was a force on the offensive line at my college, playing so well and delivering so much consistent effort that professional scouts were coming to this tiny town in West Virginia to see how good I looked in person.

Teachable Moments

When you enter a new community or even start reaching out to a new population in that community, you're going to be the new kid in town for a bit; that's just the way things work. Your heartbeat will be faster as you get the nonprofit going because you're taking a risk—the risk of moving forward into action and today's society. We realize that life is unpredictable and there are unforeseeable circumstances—like the COVID-19 pandemic—that are above any person's control. In situations like this, our basic instincts take over and we often drop into survival mode. I'm sure you've heard that term before, but do you know the science behind it? Survival mode is a result of our body's natural fight-or-flight response. It's based on the fear that we are facing death and it affects all mammals, not just the ones reading this book. In survival mode, we focus solely on staying alive, whether that's by attacking whatever we feel is threatening us or retreating from it. Sometimes survival mode can be a good thing in the short term, as it kicks us out of our doldrums and into action. But if we stay in it for too long, it causes burnout—physically, mentally, and emotionally. We can't be constantly stressed and worried about our—or our nonprofit's—minute-by-minute survival. We need time to rest, strategize, and connect to the people and the environment around us. A lot of nonprofits had to go into survival mode during the spring, summer, and fall of 2020, when their physical offices were forced to shut down and all of their in-person events were canceled. As I've said before, it's the kind of situation that almost no one had concrete plans drawn up for. Every organization deals with cancelled events once in a while, or a shutdown of the physical entity because of a disaster like a fire or a flood. But a prolonged nothingness where people couldn't even be in the same building at the same time? I can't think of anything that fits the criteria of survival mode more than that!

Survival mode meant a lot of different things to a lot of nonprofits last year. Some had to furlough or cut staff, some had to close their offices or even sell them entirely. Donations fell off and so did nonprofits' ability to keep their commitments. For many, it was a bitter pill to swallow, being unable to help people who were still very much in need, maybe even more so because of the virus and its ability to spread so rapidly.

The next move after survival mode is to figure out how to maintain the organization's operations team and sustainability. The role falls to leadership to get that consistent heartbeat going, when your nonprofit can be prepared for any situation coming down the pipe—positive or negative. The best way forward is to stand out in your community as everyone starts getting back to normal. Show them you are a leader and committed to getting things back to the way they used to be by making connections, helping those in need, and recapturing what was lost in the year of the shutdown and beyond.

The first thing that standing out in your community helps with is attracting the right businesses and individuals to join your organization. Doing so is going to open your organization up to a lot more opportunities that can drive the growth you're looking for. Your main objectives will be to deliver awareness and education to those individuals and businesses. You don't want a one-time donation from them, you want them to become part of your crusade to make your nonprofit into a success. Figure out what commonalities you have with them that can become strategic relations. How will both parties' benefit from working together and how can you grow together to get stronger and do more good over time?

Changing your organization's heartbeat from a follower to a partner to a leader takes listening. You need to know the needs of the community to get involved to the point where it's recognized that you are starting to make a difference. One of the things that always helped me before a big game or even a key practice was to meditate with a clear focus. I would shut down everything around me that might be a distraction and focus on what I was going to battle with, what I had in my arsenal, and how I would get it done.

You can do the same thing when you meditate before going into a meeting or a busy day at your office. Realize that you are the one in control of your life and of the nonprofit and consciously think about being the best version of yourself. You'll start to see the way forward to take control of your success—your impact on philanthropy, but also your lifestyle and how your career is working. To maintain that heartbeat that you want to set, you have to be resilient to effect the change you want out of the world. You have to acknowledge that change is good, even the change that we are all experiencing as we round the corner to move past COVID-19 once and for all.

That change means listening to other leaders and getting involved with their talents. When you're running a nonprofit or any type of organization, it can be tempting to just envision that you know more than everyone else and that as long as they listen to you, everything will go great. Of course, your voice is not the only one that matters, even if it is your hand that's writing the checks at the end of the day. When you involve others, not only does it broaden the potential of what can be accomplished, but you're also getting to use those other people's talents and having them expand the boundaries of what your organization can accomplish. Taking their best ideas and moving forward with them, taking the necessary risks for the bigger rewards, is how you move into that community leadership role. Now, I had an advantage in having people gravitate toward me on the football field, because even in a land full of giants, I was usually the tallest guy. Physical size might matter on the football field, but when it comes to being a community leader it's a lot more about seeing who's a fighter, who is ready to accept the challenge, and who can channel the right kind of energy to create a pathway to success that everyone can follow. When you become a person known in your community, you have the power to make positive change.

A great way to build awareness is to find similar nonprofits with the same mission and find common ways to get awareness out there. Hosting events where you can partner up with celebrities or local leaders in the community who are well known or well established is a great icebreaker as well. Focus on the mission, which should have a focal point on new donors and young people, ones who will be the future of your organization and the future of society itself. Keep giving people ways to stay plugged in, whether that is through marketing ads, social media platforms, email blasts, or press releases. Staying top of mind is a great way to stand apart.

As things start to get back to normal from the COVID-19 pandemic, there's nothing wrong with returning to the boots-on-the-ground mentality of knocking on people's doors and asking to wash their car in exchange for taking a flyer or contributing the amount of their choice. Grassroots movements are how some of the greatest causes in history have gotten their start. I can't stress enough how vital it can be to get involved in the education side of things. Figure out what your budget capacity is and start putting some of it into pamphlets and newsletters and maybe a bit of memorabilia as well. Go to the local high schools in your area and tell them you want to support or participate in pep rallies and scholarship giveaways. The education side of things is almost always part of its heartbeat and must be addressed and embraced.

At the same time, we have to adjust and adapt to society today. Millennials are getting to the age where they are entering those C-suite level jobs and having more and more impact on the organizations they work for. They are not built the same as previous generations and they don't communicate the same way, either. We have to adapt to the world of iPhones and tablets, Snapchat, Instagram, TikTok, and Twitter. We have to be able to leverage those technologies and those social media channels to get the engagement we're after. There needs to be serious research done by your organization to understand how each segment of the populations you are attempting to reach wants to be communicated with. You must find the balance between social media, in-person, and other forms of communication. That's the trend of the world. Capturing the audience on social media has to be a high priority. We have to create a way for new adults to get interested in giving back and doing things beyond what they do for compensation. Until things are 100 percent back to normal in the real world, you have to get innovative online. Try Easter egg hunts and scavenger hunts using an app. Have incentives for using the hashtags of your cause. It's a great way to really keep people interested, and that's vital when dealing with millennials; once they lose interest, it's hard to get it back. Exposure through digital media is a huge asset these days, and relatively cheap if you know how to harness it.

Proof

House of Tiny Hands' book detailing the trials and triumphs of mothers of micro-preemies has made Madelyn and her charity into a hot commodity. She is getting lots of phone calls and emails from people wanting to work with her organization, and it has reached the point where she has to consider what the right fits for her business are—you can lose a lot of that positive momentum if you hook up with a company that's not on the right side of the equation or just looking to make a splash and ride your coattails. So, before every new meeting, Madelyn makes sure to get her meditation in. She doesn't want to get swept up in her newfound celebrity and be flattered or cajoled into making deals that aren't helping the true cause of the charity in any way, shape, or form. She doesn't mind being the public face of House of Tiny Hands in order to get it more recognition, but she knows the nonprofit's needs must always come first and rise above her own interests. Thus, she takes the compliments with grace but ensures that she keeps directing the focus back to how each company she meets can form a relationship that drives home the mission statements of House of Tiny Hands in innovative, positive ways.

She looks for events to co-sponsor, such as fun runs and silent auctions, and anything where people are going to donate freely without needing some sort of catch as an incentive to open their hands to the community. When a magazine wants her to participate in a "Most Eligible Bachelorettes" photoshoot and layout, she turns them down—it's flattering, but it's not going to get the foundation any further along the path to its goals. However, she will appear on podcasts and TV forums and radio interviews to talk about society's ills and how to push past the coronavirus environment and feel safe again. Any chance she has to disseminate more and more knowledge to new audiences is an opportunity worth taking. She'll try to turn a single appearance into a regular spot and use her knowledge of all thing's children-related to make herself a marketable repeat guest. If she's good on camera, she'll be even better in front of a crowd, and that can get her speaking engagements around the city and throughout the region. Getting involved with the local government and its many outreach efforts will expand that part of her status as a subject-matter expert (SME) as well. From there, it's making sure that she is not the only bright star shining in her charity's solar system. She can use her recognition to bring it to other people in her organization: volunteers who are going above and beyond; families who have used the nonprofit's resources to get through tough times and excel; and even donors (if they are willing to take the spotlight), calling attention to their philanthropy. When she puts on events, they shouldn't be about fancy dresses and lavish ballrooms, but about drawing attention to the cause in a format that will make people want to be part of something larger than themselves, something that makes them feel good to contribute to, no matter what form that contribution takes.

CHAPTER 4

Sports Journey

The journey is often the most underrated part of a trip. When you take the cross-country trek from your home state to Disney World, not very many people are pumped to go driving across Louisiana and Mississippi for hours on end when they know that Splash Mountain and Pirates of the Caribbean are waiting down the road. The thing is though, the journey is what really builds you up to succeed and be your best self when you make it to your destination. Consider your own academic career. Whatever job you have now might have been something you were already thinking about when you entered high school, but there is no way you were ready to do that job when you were 14 years old. The experiences that take you from a bright-eyed teenager to a college graduate outstanding in your field are powerful, enlightening, and absolutely necessary. The sports part of the journey is specific to my story, but I do believe that anyone who has been on a similar path will have no problem identifying the key points of the journey I took—from believing my future was in football to thinking completely the opposite, to finding a balance that led me to gathering all the tools I would eventually need to find my true calling in life.

TRANSITION

My Story

My senior year of college was a huge one—I was getting my master's and getting prepared for the NFL. I was going to have to make a choice between getting in shape for the NFL draft or taking an opportunity to go to Shanghai, China, for a year of international business school as an internship. It was an incredible choice to make, but I never doubted the way to make the decision; I prayed to God to give me inspiration on which pathway to take. I pursued graduate school but never let up on my training.

Even after I made that decision, I wasn't sure it was the right choice. Fortunately, I realized that it was not a decision I had to make solely by myself. My family was there to counsel me when I couldn't quite find my way. The pastor at my church, a great man named Bruce Hogan, did as well. They encouraged me not to quit on my dream of playing pro football. They told me this crisis of faith was a wake-up call to get more serious, and I made my decision to set my master's degree aside for a year to focus on trying to make my football dream come true.

I had used football as a gateway to become educated. But that didn't mean I couldn't still pursue my goals and dreams in the sport. I realized that my chances of getting drafted coming out of a division II school were very small, but I still wanted to take a shot in the NFL. I didn't want to be twenty years down the road asking myself what might have been. So, I gave up the internship and packed up my stuff in 2009 and moved back to Florida. There was a team right in my old backyard that was getting ready to have tryouts for walk-ons. It was time to see if I had what it took to be a Miami Dolphin.

As soon as I got back home, I connected with a lot of local guys, including an agent, and headed for the Dolphins' camp to start working out. I was focused on three things—training, process, and protocol, getting my mind ready to make something happen. We worked out at the ESPN facility, and I did pretty good. I competed; I did my thing; I had a good coach who treated me like everyone else out there, even though most of them had been drafted and I had not. I got signed to the team and spent the 2010 season with them. Tony Sparano was the head coach that season, and he really inspired me in a lot of ways. The way he spoke and the way he ran the organization, it made me want to keep playing. It didn't work out with the Dolphins, but I was not ready to give up yet.

I had worked hard and still believed in myself, so I went to Canada and spent some time with the Montreal Alouettes of the Canadian Football League (CFL). There I played for Coach Marc Trestman, who was inspiring. He had a way of relating to players that I had never seen on any level of competition before. It was not my best performance on the field, unfortunately. I was pretty sure my career was over at that point, but my agent called and said he knew of one more shot for me, and that was with the Pittsburgh Steelers. I got my plane ticket, made my way to Pennsylvania, and went straight to training camp. I had only been there a few days when I started struggling one day in practice. I got really dehydrated and wound up collapsing at practice. They loaded me into an ambulance and took me to the hospital. I can barely remember any of it, just a vague sense of looking out the windows of the ambulance as I was rushed to the hospital. Nobody knew what was going on other than a diagnosis of dehydration. At one point I looked up and there were 16 different doctors huddled around my bed trying to make sense of it all.

Eventually, they figured it out—I had a blood clot in my leg. My circulatory system wasn't working the way it should. The doctors told me straight that my two choices were to have my leg amputated or to remove the clot via surgery. They gave me sedatives to relax me and put me to sleep and everything got dark.

The surgery took 16 hours as they tried to release the blood clot before it became fatal. While I was on the operating table, my heart stopped, and I died. While I was dead, all I knew was that something serious was going on. I had a dark epiphany at that moment, like my mind was in a state of unconsciousness but I could still feel the real world. The doctors were able to start my heart back up. I felt like I was going to make it through if I just trusted God to see it through. The next morning, I woke up and the first thing I saw was my family. My parents and my sisters had come, and I just totally broke down. At that moment I knew for sure that life was more important than the game of football, but football had probably saved my life. If I hadn't been in such good shape, I would have not made it. They had used an EKG to shock my heart back to life and I didn't really understand it when I woke up; all I saw were these giant bandages on my leg. They explained I had gone through a huge trauma, and it was time to give up the cleats once and for all.

I was in the hospital for the next three months. They released me from the hospital in a wheelchair with a pair of crutches. I had been rolled into the hospital at 350 pounds and left Pittsburgh at 280 pounds. It wasn't just my body that needed fixing, either. I was in a different spot mentally. But I knew I had to treat rehab just how I had treated every element of my football career—by being consistent and attacking what was in front of me. I had to rebuild myself. I have no doubt that my work ethic got me through rehab faster than most people would have gotten through it. I spent hours and hours a day stretching, bending my knee, walking, and eventually jogging. My new home away from home was the Pinecrest Physical Facility, and my new best friend was an amazing trainer named Kevin, who was a big part of my recovery and an absolute inspiration. He always challenged me; he knew I had it in me to have a faster recovery because of the way I focused. He worked with me every single day. Simply an amazing person at a time when that was exactly what I needed. I had lost a lot of my body's firepower in those three months and could tell football was really over for me.

Teachable Moments

Hopefully, your nonprofit will never reach a moment of life or death, but situations like the COVID-19 pandemic of 2020 prove that they can happen. It's in those moments that you have to realize that what you thought was going to be the definition of your charity might not be what happens after all. I thought I'd be an offensive lineman in the NFL for 10 years before I had to decide on my next career. Turns out that choice got made for me, but it didn't dent my desire to find something I was passionate about. When your nonprofit faces that big decision, that's the time for you to get humble and put aside your wants and needs for those of the most important people in your organization—the ones that you created the charity to help and the ones who work for you. The charity never really belongs to us, but to those we serve.

I like to think of it the way you would if you were an interior designer. You can have ideas that everyone loves and that you think is the chicest thing in the world, but if your client wants something completely different that you think is hideous, who is right? The answer, of course, is the client. It's their house and their dime, you're just the one facilitating the vision that satisfies them. The same is true for a nonprofit. You might have big dreams of becoming a keynote speaker around the state and being hailed as a great innovator in your field, but if COVID-19 or some other unforeseen circumstance changes that idea, you need to roll with the punches and figure out how else to serve.

The number one strategy is being able to step back from your own viewpoint and understand where the need is in your community as it relates to your specific charitable endeavor. You might have started out wanting to raise funds for inner-city children to all get their own Chromebooks to take home from school, only to find out that a third of them can barely read or write at grade level, much less use a computer. So, you pivot away from your partnership with Google and instead make one with a local tutoring company or start stumping for donations from local bookstores to get more texts into kids' hands. What is going to make the people you serve safer, better, happier, or have their needs met more consistently? That is not only the most important question—it should be the only question worth answering when your nonprofit is in the transition away from its original calling card.

Proof

The success of House of Tiny Hands' mothers' book has taken the nonprofit in a new direction and CEO Madelyn isn't going to let the momentum go to waste. She starts making the charity into more of a community of parents of micro-preemies to be the true voices that lead the way, going as far as to create a leadership council to help her keep the ship on the right course as the charity gains more and more attention. Her worst fear is that the message gets twisted, and the organization starts caring more about how much money it can raise than how to help the individual, like some mega-churches she has seen. She never wants her organization to go on automatic pilot. She always wants to present the picture of an intimate enough setting that a scared pregnant woman who wonders what will happen if she delivers her baby early will be able to walk into the office; join the group chat; respond to a DM line on Twitter; or simply pick up the phone and reach a comforting, knowledgeable voice for information and support. When the pivotal moment is upon her, she doesn't try to simply touch up her business plan, she tears it up and rewrites it entirely. The same work and diligence that went into the original version have to be recreated here, from her role as CEO all the way down to the policy on office supplies.

THE CALLING

My Story

What makes you passionate about what you're passionate about? It's sort of a paradox to try and unravel that mystery. When I've talked to younger people, I've told them that somewhere along the way they're going to hit on something that they're passionate about and that never feels like work to them, and when they do, they'll know what their calling is. As recently as a decade ago, I was convinced that my calling was either busting free running backs on the football field or racking up revenue in the business world. Now here I am today writing this book and it turns out the answer was neither. I think a lot of my passion has to do with the neighborhood I grew up in. Some were scary, some were protective, and some you didn't know what was going to happen from one day to the next. The ones where I made true friends, where there were healthy activities to engage my time with, and where my family was able to contribute to an overall brighter future were the ones that shaped me best for future success. I had that sense of community for years on the football field and in some of my best classes, but it's a tenuous thing. College is all about preparing for the next thing, but sometimes that transition takes you away from the things you like best. Once I had to give up on my NFL dream, I moved back home to South Florida and the Miami area. My family was facing a financial crisis and had a lot of bills due. We were running low on resources, so I transitioned to the business world because I knew I could make some money to provide support and take care of my family. Rebuilding was an important step in reestablishing a good balance. I was blessed to find something in corporate sales and really did well, with opportunities to travel to Europe and spend two months working in downtown London. It allowed me to expand my vision beyond football and strengthen my legacy, supporting my generation. Finding ways to balance my life, increase my value toward other people, and add value to their lives—with the critical decisions being made to assist them—was very valuable to me, and I think set the path to where I am now.

Teachable Moments

The calling is something you often hear in terms of people entering the ministry to serve others by strengthening their connection to God. I believe it is critical to feel called to get involved with a nonprofit organization because being involved in one is counterintuitive to pretty much everything that the average person is motivated by. If you're going to start a nonprofit, you're pretty much saying goodbye to any sort of normal paycheck, working hours, benefits, or vacations for the foreseeable future. You have to be called to something to do that willingly. The only people that work those kinds of hours for that kind of pay are typically entrepreneurs who are hoping that all that hard work is going to result in a huge payday or several of them down the road. You know that payday isn't coming if you're in the nonprofit game, and if you are after that, you're definitely in the wrong line of work!

The calling to make a difference in others' lives is a rare gift. For most people, they are willing to help others after they've helped themselves and their own. If there's time left, they'll be part of a monthly blood drive or contribute to a GoFundMe after seeing a sad story on social media or something like that, and that's awesome. If it weren't for that sort of human compassion, charities would fall by the wayside. But for the people who burn with that desire to help every single day of the year, that's where nonprofits come into play. But it can't be just about helping nonstop; you have to be able to find a balance that is going to make you successful. That means not just being able to be a problem solver, but also finding out how to manage relationships with your employees, your volunteers, your community partners, and the people your charity was designed to help the most. Being able to establish a good rapport and build the right balance on your team are essential goals to putting them in positions of growth and building on their strengths.

Proof

At House of Tiny Hands, Madelyn's leadership council is becoming more and more of a workforce to be proud of, using its strengths to find new avenues for the charity to connect with its community. While everyone loves the cute babies, they realize that they're missing a huge component in the story of micro preemies—the long-term success. A call goes out on social media groups and through the community portal for adults who were born before 30 weeks' gestation or under five pounds of birth weight. The response is sudden and magnificent. People from all walks of life come forward with their stories to tell and their social circles rise up around them, many hearing their stories for the first time. Madelyn takes a step back to simply serve as an administrator; she lets her leadership council steer the ship more and more as she focuses on keeping the infrastructure intact, while the community recovers from COVID-19 and elbow bumps and masks start to give way to big smiles and hugs once again. She starts to reintroduce physical get-togethers and small social events, creating a balance between the newfound success online and the undeniable spirit of standing face to face with someone, hearing their story, reading their body language, and letting them know that they have your support.

TRUE PURPOSE

My Story

When things start to happen, when you're enjoying your lifestyle and career balance, you just never know what to expect outside of those. There could be many, many more opportunities that open up, and who knows where they could direct you? I had to figure out the next best move for me to make was once I was making good money, gaining experience, and helping my family get back to a place of stability. I had a master's degree in business administration and leadership. I knew that I was able to do more and have an impact on society. My ability to make a difference was very important and played a huge role in how I was moving forward. When I realized that every day was not going to be focused on lifting weights and playing the game, that was a scary thought in and of itself. But when I realized I could accomplish so much more from the other experiences I had had growing up, off the field, and in those first few years as a professional, I knew I was able to put more out there by simply being part of a new community.

It didn't happen overnight for me, of course. I doubt it does for anyone. But just like when I started getting really comfortable on the offensive line, there started being moments where I was finding my way to something that I knew I could really do well, and it just started to click. I knew how finances worked and how corporations formed and put together a sound organization. I knew a lot of small nonprofits and charitable startup organizations struggle mightily with those concepts, often to the point where it destroys them before they ever have a chance to get out and do something great. I really wanted to be a professional in that space. I was a financial adviser who was fascinated by charitable planning, how organizations work, and what a successful organization looks like versus one that is just in the beginning phases. Helping others really inspired me to be an agent of change. I became passionate about applying my knowledge of finances to the philanthropic world. It's sort of an odd thing; a lot of people that get into that business aren't the strongest when it comes to finances and how to properly raise and spend money. They have all the passion in the world for making a difference, but the little things are what keep them from doing it to the best of their abilities.

Teachable Moments

How do you find your true purpose and, perhaps more specifically, how do you find your organization's true purpose? I'm a big believer in meditation, especially in the crazy world we're living in. How much time per day do you have to just sit and be and think things through? Try to count those minutes up and I bet you will find there are horrifyingly few. I'm talking about a time when you're completely alone and distraction-free: no texts, no phone calls, no notifications on your phone, nobody knocking on your door, no TV on, no spouse or child or roommate in your ear. Just you. If I don't get my meditation time every morning, my day is a lot more stressful and disorganized than it would be otherwise. But when I get those 15-30 minutes of utter peace and relaxation, my mind clarifies things in ways that I doubt I ever could reach without it.

It's in meditation that I not only solve some of my biggest problems but come up with ideas that I doubt I would have been able to conceive of otherwise. It is in those moments that your heart will really speak to you and things will become crystal clear on your best path forward. Now you can't just sit there, you have to challenge yourself to think clearly on what the best situation is for you and for your organization. What are your strengths? What can you do better than anyone else? How can you harness that into helping other people? Whatever that skill is, that's your gateway into nonprofit success. It has to burn bright enough that you can deliver that vision to other people and get them on board. They might never have the precise passion that you do, but that's OK. If they believe in you and you believe in the path, that can be enough. Hard workers are always going to give you remarkable efforts because accomplishing goals is what drives their inner success.

Proof

As House of Tiny Hands evolves, CEO Madelyn spends more and more time thinking about the organization's legacy. She employs a legion of volunteers who all have a direct tie to the micro-preemie community: medical professionals, moms, and micro-preemies who have grown up to lead wonderful lives. There is an amazing number of stories that have been told and continue to be told. Madelyn is so joyous to see Miami coming together on these amazing causes when she realizes that she no longer wants to limit this incredible sense of community and compassion to South Beach.

It happens one day while she's meditating before work in her home office, with soothing sounds of the ocean and birds chirping coming through the window. She has her assistant screen most of the stories she gets from micro-preemie moms and was just in love with one story from a woman who had micro-preemie twin girls born at just 23 weeks, the same as Madelyn herself. The woman's twins had to be separated at nine days of life because one of them suffered a perforated intestine that required a medical procedure at a larger, more capable hospital. The problem was that hospitals were 30 minutes away from each other, which meant the woman and her husband spent the next four months taking turns splitting their time and being stretched thin by the commutes and the lack of time for each baby. Eventually, both babies got back to their home hospital and then went home. It really touched Madelyn's heart and she desperately wanted to tell the woman's story, but there was one problem. The story had taken place in Texas, not South Florida, which was the scope of House of Tiny Hands. At the time, it had just seemed like a case of tough luck. Now the thought struck Madelyn like a bolt of lightning. She had an online portal that was based in Miami, but by no means did it have to stay there. She could open its doors and its resources to anyone in the US who wanted to share their journey and needed resources, and by doing so she could evolve House of Tiny Hands into a nationwide organization, still based in Miami, but with the power to connect to hospitals and children's groups all over the country to better educate and support micro-preemie families. At long last, her true calling had been discovered.

CHAPTER 5

Philanthropy

The idea of philanthropy in general is something that separates us from the rest of God's creatures. We seek to help those less fortunate than we are and use our resources, our wealth, and our energy to make it happen. Some animal species might adopt an orphan out of maternal instincts, but I guarantee you there's never been a cheetah that ran down two gazelle on a Tuesday morning that thinks to itself, "You know, those cheetahs that live across the plain looked hungry this morning, I think I'll give them my second gazelle."

Our government system started with philanthropy. A community grows as we reinvest in it. We build better schools to attract successful people to the community so that their children can grow up with good education and contribute vital things to the same community. When everyone has food on the table, a roof over their heads, and a job to go to in the morning, our crime rate goes down, our unemployment rate goes down, there are more dollars to spend on the infrastructure, and all facets of life go more smoothly. Better care for our fellow man equals a better community, a better quality of life, and a better experience for everyone. But it doesn't happen overnight. It takes engagement at all levels and from all angles to make it work.

FINANCIAL SERVICES

My Story

As I've mentioned before, I had a knack for making money growing up. I worked at Taco Bell in high school even though other people that worked there seem to think I should be doing something better. When I was going to college in West Virginia, I started working at Dick's Sporting Goods selling weight machines. It was a perfect fit for them because if you're going to have someone selling exercise equipment to people, the six-foot seven-inch, 320-pound offensive lineman who's built like an armored truck is a pretty good salesman. Money makes the world go round and I found that out pretty quickly as I moved past my football days and into my life as a financial professional. I needed to produce to take care of my family and to reciprocate all the things they had done for me over many, many years. Taking care of family is how you guarantee your legacy and how you plan for their future and for your own. When I started to really key in on nonprofit consulting as the future of my career, it really tipped me off to the idea that my experience made me a difference-maker. It is a role I relish because so many times I get a call or an email or a text from a firm saying, "We've got a great idea. We know what we want to do, but we just can't turn the finances around. We don't know where to cut costs on our operating budget, we don't know how to keep the flow going on donations, and we don't know how to plan for the future." That's vital for any business, but specifically for one that is so utterly reliable on donations and giving. It's not like most organizations also own a restaurant or sell smartphones on the side. If it's not coming in from generous donors and corporate partnerships, you're going to have to get creative.

Teachable Moments

Of course, getting creative, as you know from your own experience running a nonprofit and as we have seen in real and fictional examples throughout this book, is the name of the game. You're not competing for things people want, you're competing for their sense of compassion and charity. But there are other ways to raise money if you know how to use the right tools.

The first thing to know about is the concept of operating reserves, which are pretty much what they sound like. Your operating budget is all the money you have earmarked for use over the current financial year; the reserves are any unrestricted surpluses that are available to be used at the discretion of the nonprofit's board of directors. You might think of this as your rainy day fund because its presence allows you to take on unplanned or unexpected additional costs that result when something changes in your organization, your environment, or the circumstances by which you collect funds. When the country enters a massive recession, as it did in 2008-2010; or there's a localized natural disaster such as an earthquake or a hurricane that shifts focus away from your cause for a length of time; or, obviously, an event like COVID-19 occurs and all of your planned events dry up for a while, you still have funds available to keep yourself afloat.

The presence of this fund doesn't just keep the lights on at your office; it also promotes public confidence and confidence from your donors that you are a strong organization capable of weathering storms on your own. It gives them the sense that you are a reliable part of the community that deserves their support. The ability to have excess funds often takes some nonprofit start-ups by surprise. They envision that every dollar they collect must be spent. However, that's not the case. The difference is that surpluses for a nonprofit must simply remain with the corporation itself, rather than going to shareholders or individuals as it would in a for-profit business. If you only have enough money in the tank to get you through the current month, it's going to significantly limit your nonprofit's ability to plan long term and commit to future endeavors with other organizations, government offices, and so forth. Your operating reserves are those funds designated as unrestricted net assets that are available for use in emergencies to sustain financial operations in the unanticipated event of significant unbudgeted increases in operating expenses or the loss of operating revenue. There are three types, detailed below:

Board-Designated: Defined as the portion of your available unrestricted net assets that the board has designated as operating reserves. These are typically in the form of cash, near-cash, and low-risk investments such as bonds. Access to these funds requires board approval.

Undesignated: These are funds that are not given a specific purpose. If they are depleted, the board-designated operating reserves can be used as an internal line of credit during the year. These funds are part of the available unrestricted net assets of an organization that have not been designated by the board for other specific purposes. Keeping funds in this designation is not recommended.

Available unrestricted net assets: These are the simplest form of assets kept by the organization and are often used to fund the operating reserves at the end of each fiscal year. They are defined as the portion of the total unrestricted net assets available for designation by the board for operating reserves and non-operational special purposes of board-designated endowments that further the mission of the organization.

One of these is to use life insurance to leave a much grander legacy for your charity. A whole life insurance[3] policy covers someone for their entire life as long as the premiums are paid. This is different from term insurance, which expires after a certain amount of time. Whole life insurance pays out upon a person's death the whole amount to the designation of their choice. While a person's family is foremost in their mind when creating such a policy, for independently wealthy people, such as members of your board of directors or those who frequently contribute, this sort of policy can be the solution for someone who wants to make a lasting donation that will far outstrip what they might be able to contribute year to year. For instance, if a donor takes out a whole life insurance policy with your charity as the beneficiary, they might be able to get a payout of $100,000 on premiums of $100-$200 per month. Even if they are generous enough to donate $5,000 a year to your cause, it would take 20 years to reach the same legacy amount as what could be accomplished by only paying those much smaller premiums on a month-to-month basis.

It is something you yourself can consider based on your current family situation, your age, and your financial health.

A second tool that you should consider is the 501(h) election. Federal tax laws allow every charity to engage in some lobbying activities in their state and federal legislative bodies. There are limits in place that keep nonprofits from spending all their time

---

3   Whole Life insurance is intended to provide death benefit protection for an individual's entire life. With payment of the required guaranteed premiums, you will receive a guaranteed death benefit and guaranteed cash values inside the policy. Guarantees are based on the claims-paying ability of the issuing insurance company.

and money in lobbying, but part of the Internal Revenue Code of 1934 says that it can be allowed as long as it's "insubstantial" to your charity's overall activities. Using inexpensive techniques like volunteerism or social media activity, you can get a lot done in a tax-exempt format, which will lead to big savings for your charity come April 15. This allows you to be a little more sophisticated than just grassroots movements in your local district. You can apply that cash to your local government, to the state government, or even all the way to Washington D.C. if you choose.

Another avenue that can be of great aid to charities is the concept of a donor-advised fund (DAF). A DAF is a simple, tax-efficient, and flexible way for individuals to give to their favorite charities; in fact, its sole purpose is to act as a charitable investment account. When a person contributes cash, securities, or other assets to a DAF at a public charity, they are eligible to take an immediate tax deduction. They can then invest those funds for tax-free growth or recommend grants to any IRS-qualified public charity. When you give donations, you typically want them to be effective as soon as possible. Donor-advised funds are the most rapidly growing charitable financial vehicle in the country because they are easy to use and tax-favorable. Let's take a closer look at how they work.

First, you make a tax-deductible donation. This can be in the form of cash, stocks, or non-publicly traded assets such as private business interests, private company stock, or even cryptocurrency. A contribution to a DAF is a commitment to the charity that cannot be returned to the donor or any other individual for any purpose other than giving the grant to a charity. You can donate restricted stock, life insurance policies, oil and gas royalty interests, retirement assets, pre-IPO shares, hedge fund interests, private equity, LLC and Limited Partnership interest, private company

S-corporation stock, private company C-corporation stocks, publicly traded stocks, mutual fund shares, and bonds. While you are deciding which charities to support, your donation has the potential to grow, making available more money for charities. Organizations that offer DAFs have many layers and ranges of investment options from which you can select an investment strategy for your charitable investment. These will vary from firm to firm.

Once you have your DAF set up, you can support any IRS-qualified public charity with the recommendations from it. This means anything from your church to your alma mater, to the local soup kitchen, to a children's hospital. The choice is entirely up to you. If you're running a charity and you have generous donors who want to give the gift that truly keeps on giving, this is a tremendous suggestion to make to them. If you have a charity in mind and you are not 100 percent sure about its claims to legitimacy, know that the public charity that sponsors your account will conduct its own due diligence to ensure that the funds granted go to an IRS qualifier and will be used strictly for charitable purposes. No dollar you invest will go somewhere that you don't want it to.

Here are some things a donor-advised fund allows you to do:

- *Contribute from a wide range of assets*: Giving via cash or credit card can limit how much you give. Contributing assets other than cash is made simple with a DAF and can be done with the click of a button, turning your smart investments into much-needed contributions to your favorite charities.

- *Maximize your potential tax benefits*: If you donate cash via a wire transfer or a check, you're eligible for an income tax deduction of up to 60 percent of your adjusted gross income (AGI). If you donate long-term appreciated securities directly to a charity, you can maximize your tax benefit and the overall amount you can grant to charity. In this instance, you can become eligible for an income tax deduction of the full fair-market value of the asset, up to 30 percent of your AGI, and eliminate capital gains tax on long-term appreciated assets as long as they've been held for longer than 365 days.

- *Use your donation to invest with tax-free growth*: Once you have supplied the necessary requirements to your donor-advised fund, you can recommend an investment strategy to grow your account and make even more dollars for the charity. Many of these funds allow you to nominate your own financial advisor to oversee the investment of the charitable funds.

- *Organize and keep records easily*: When you use a donor-advised fund, you don't have to keep track of all the gift acknowledgments from the charity, just the receipt for your fund contributions. It makes it far easier to account for everything come tax time.

- *Promote legacy planning*: Donor-advised funding can be a part of legacy planning as a bequest in a person's will for the DAF sponsor. This can support one charity or many, and these gifts will eliminate or greatly reduce the estate tax sale that a person's heirs end up taking on otherwise.

Proof

The more House of Tiny Hands grows, the more Madelyn hopes to spread an integral part of her vision: that hospitals can make the commitment to resuscitating babies who are born before 24 weeks gestation. She admits that she loves getting into discussions about this subject with hospital administrators and healthcare system boards. When they tell her how much they admire her cause but that they don't believe spending money on babies that young and immature is worth the investment, she hits them with a roundhouse punch: that without the vision to resuscitate baby's pre-24 weeks, there would be no House of Tiny Hands. You see, Madelyn was born at 23 weeks and five days maturity. She knows it's not exactly fair to make it so personal, but the looks of incredulity she often gets when those officials realize what she means and what her true story is have made the difference more than a few times.

But Madelyn can't possibly meet every hospital administrator in the country one on one. She needs to generate something with legs that can stand on its own and be a voice louder than hers. She needs a champion; actually, more than one will be even better. She's done great locally in Miami and the hospitals in town know who she is and what agenda she's striving for. But go as few as 200 miles north to Orlando and she's just another crusader trying to change minds one at a time. So, she takes advantage of the 501(h) election and begins converting some of the charity's donations into political capital—tentatively, at first. She attends a fundraiser for a state senator who she knows had a preemie born at 30 weeks and bends her ear for 20 minutes about the cause. The senator agrees to bringing it up in a committee meeting at the state capitol the following month.

MENTORING

My Story

I didn't have a natural mentor growing up. My parents were amazing and taught me lots of life lessons, there is no doubt of that, but that natural connection didn't seem to happen until I was well into my college career. Sometimes I reflect on that and wonder what might have gone differently if I had someone to pattern my life after when I was that wayward kid moving from state to state and sport to sport not really understanding what was going to come next. My high school coaches were too obsessed with getting me up to speed to make a real difference, and I can't really blame them.

My college coaches were equal parts helpful and frustrating. They taught me a lot about football, but they seemed to have no interest in helping me navigate life. I hate to think it was because of my race, but the more years that have gone by since then, the more obvious it seems that this was exactly their problem with me. I had slipped through the cracks of Division I football because of my family's lack of knowledge about the recruiting process and had landed at this smaller school. The coaches seemed to take umbrage with that and believe that I should have been this unstoppable Superman on the field. When I struggled or when I was injured, they treated me like garbage, and it became hard to respect men who looked down on me and didn't fulfill their end of the coach-player relationship.

My best mentor came in business school, as I've mentioned previously, and really opened my eyes to a lot of the way the world worked outside a college campus and a football field. But when I moved into the private sector as an adult, I decided that kids needed more than I had received, and I got into the Big Brothers Big Sisters of America program. I know it's for the kids, but it absolutely developed my personal growth in various ways and enriched my soul and spirit, allowing me to see the greater good of giving and sharing experiences. Seeing my mentee benefit and get the satisfaction of experiences he might otherwise have missed out entirely on was a huge plus and let me see the good that one person can do with small, concerted efforts in the life of someone else. You never realize how crucial it can be to have someone to lean on until you give them that opportunity and see how much they can flourish with just a few stolen moments a day.

Teachable Moments

Tough times can get people down, no matter how optimistic your volunteers or how inspiring the speeches you give at the weekly staff meeting are.

If you're new to the startup game or to the area you're working in, finding someone who has that experience can be a breath of fresh air and a life raft for you as you stumble along looking to do the right thing as much as possible. It doesn't matter how old you are or what level of education you have, a mentor doesn't have to be the end-all, be-all in your decision-making process. Just having a sounding board to toss your best or worst ideas off and see how they reverberate is a great cause for finding someone. When you have a mentor, you become better at analyzing your ways with other and newer perspectives.

To get people to believe in your cause and to believe in themselves takes a more personal touch, something that helps them navigate the bumpy road that nonprofits are often on. Learn to be a great storyteller in your one-on-one conversations with people in your organization and in the community at large. While you are a mentee, it's great to also be a mentor. You'll likely find your most adroit, effective volunteers are people on their way up the ladder toward their own great causes. Help shape them while they are in your same orbit by offering them your own tricks of the trade. As in most relationships in the nonprofit world, you'll likely learn as much as you teach.

Proof

Madelyn considers herself an expert when it comes to getting things done in Miami, but the world is a lot bigger than South Beach. To make sure she's not in over her head, she wants someone who has run a larger charity board to ask for advice from now and again. That ends up being a former mayor's wife, who took her own charity across the entire Gulf Coast years ago and has since retired but is still active in the philanthropic and social circles. It's nothing formal; lunch or coffee every week or two to get some much-needed face time in a relaxed environment coupled with a lot of texting, usually late at night when Madelyn is always convinced her mentor will be sleeping, but she never is. The mentor encourages Madelyn to pay it forward and she does, creating an internship in the nonprofit designed for a college student who is interested in running charitable organizations. Madelyn picks the recipient herself each year and puts them to work, letting them shadow most of her engagements and day-to-day life. For those who she warrants deserve the honor, she takes them out of town on a business trip once per summer. She encourages diversity in the applications but reminds everyone that only the best of the best will get the opportunity. Even if the chosen few end up on a different career path, Madelyn is hopeful they'll be more sympathetic to nonprofits as a result.

COMMUNITY ENGAGEMENT

My Story

I don't have to remind you that I never felt part of a great community in my youth. New York City was electric but had its highs and lows, and I was too young to be involved in much of anything. My first stay in Florida was mostly about goofing around with my friends and having fun, which resulted in our relocation to Haiti. The Haitian community mostly consisted of us hoping to get back home behind our high fences without seeing a dead body or being kidnapped. Then I was tossed back into the Florida atmosphere at the most pivotal time of a young person's life—the beginning of high school—knowing absolutely no one. I began building a sense of community in the football locker room and the classrooms of my college, but even those chafed when I was confronted with racism and prejudice at unexpected times from unexpected sources.

Eventually, as an adult, I realized that to take part in community engagement, I had to create it; I started with my own family's financial woes and expanded slowly outward. Going from watching out for yourself, to watching out for your neighbors, to watching out for your community is such a powerful, revelatory experience. Imagine standing alone in a street with a bulldozer coming right at you, with the words "poverty" and "crime" written on the side of it. You might be big and strong like I am, but next to a bulldozer? I'm tiny and weak. You know you're going to give it a good fight and you're determined to battle, but you know it's really just a matter of time until it wipes the floor with you. Except when it gets closer, you don't start to lose control. You look to your left, and there's your neighbor standing arm in arm with you. You look to your right, and there's the small business owner from around the corner. You realize they are supporting you, and that you are supporting them too. As the bulldozer gets even closer, you realize there's not just the three of you, but a whole community of support barring the path of destruction. One person can't stop bad things in a community, but a community can do anything: stop crime, kick out gangs, stomp out drug abuse, improve literacy rates, or cut down the unemployment rates. ANYTHING.

Teachable Moments

The COVID-19 pandemic of 2020 that stretched into 2021 for most of the world was one long teachable moment when it came to community engagement. That's what happens when you are no longer allowed to be in the same room with people, hug or kiss them, shake hands, or smile, and when you have to stand six feet apart as if there were an invisible force field around each and every one of us.

We were extremely lucky to be living in a time when technology allowed us to see each other and exchange ideas in real time with video conferencing. When I was growing up, that technology didn't exist outside of *The Jetsons*, but in the past decade, it's become a huge step forward in real-time interaction without needing to take a train, a bus, a car, or a plane to get there. The ability to speak to members of their own organizations, volunteers, donors, and more kept some nonprofits from going under or going insane during the first few fearful months of the coronavirus lockdown. It also allowed many of my clients to remain sustainable when the early days looked like that was going to be extraordinarily difficult to achieve.

While I wouldn't wish this pandemic and its auxiliary circumstances on anyone, even my worst enemy, there's no doubt that a silver lining of getting people to invest and trust wholeheartedly in digital technology did emerge as a result. It allowed organizations that had been operating within a set pattern for decades to realize the power of digital marketing and online social media platforms. The best part was it wasn't just a quick fix; they realized that these technologies were valuable tools that could be used regardless of the climate outside to position themselves online, reach completely different audiences, and concoct a sustainable business model that could be run with enough cash reserves to be better prepared for when the next interruption rolled around. The digital revolution for nonprofits is like few other niches in the world. Finding ways to connect with community members, getting them informed and organized, and being able to see what other organizations are doing and emulate them are all huge tools to use during a time of crisis, whether it's just for your organization or something widespread. Digital technology creates a two-way street of communication for any nonprofit that is open 24/7, 365 days a year.

It's no surprise that many organizations were underprepared and found out the hard way that nothing was guaranteed—not facilities or social events or donor dollars—when the world suddenly turned uncertain.

If you have strong community ties, you can reinvent how your nonprofit works because you can tap into your community and find out what it needs. You can give your donors the ability to voice their concerns on how they want to see the charity go forward in uncertain times. That doesn't mean it should turn into mob rule. But connecting with your donors who suddenly can't attend fundraisers, luncheons, and black-tie affairs is a huge luxury to have when you can't step foot in the same room as them.

While it wasn't always pleasant, the pandemic also allowed some organizations to trim the fat on their budgets and separate what was necessary to run the organization from what was redundant. In some cases, this meant reducing staff; in others, it meant downsizing office space; and in still others, it came down to the realization that things like a graphic design department or a PR firm were not needed when said work could be given to freelancers or volunteers. That isn't fun to deal with, especially if you're taking away someone's livelihood, but the bottom line and the charity itself must remain priorities at all times. The money spent paying someone's salary to do a non-essential task could easily be repurposed into more funds for a cause or better resources for the people your organization is trying to serve the most.

Many donors are key in regard to the growth and retention of organizations. The resources that donors provide offer a lot more flexibility in running management and operations infrastructure without being disrupted.

Connecting virtually has really provided the gateway of connection. This proves to be one of the best ways to continue to promote and bring value to the community, host town halls and meetings, engage with the community, and provide strategic value.

Donors advise on funds, democratizing philanthropy to change the world. The US philanthropic landscape is transforming; new generations of individual donors' control and impact giving programs at a time when the concerted philanthropic effort is needed to meet the UN Sustainable Development Goals (SDGs).

Millennials are looking for giving opportunities that provide clear benefits and can demonstrate impact, given the demands on their attention and time. It's clear that the solution to engaging this critical group of individual donors must include making it easy to give and providing means to long-term philanthropic engagement. Typical comments from interviewees include, "I wish I could do more, but I don't know how," and, "Our generation has been taught to save for education, but not to save for philanthropy." One woman told us she knew she wanted to do something to combat sex trafficking but didn't know where to start. A single mom with two kids in school, she did not have time to do research. If women like her were presented with more accessible, strategic ways to give, they would respond in significant numbers.

The international community faces a wide array of challenges, including climate change, poverty, malnutrition, and gender inequality; given the prevalence and severity of these issues, there is widespread recognition that the nonprofit public and private sectors must come together to address them at the global level. The major framework and focus for action are the UN-led Sustainable Development Goals, also known as the Global Goals. In September 2015, 193 countries unanimously approved the adoption of 17 sustainable development goals to be achieved by 2030. The goals are intended to galvanize action worldwide through concrete targets for poverty reduction, food security, human health, education, climate change mitigation, and a range of other objectives across economic, social, and environmental pillars. The SDGs represent an unprecedented commitment to solving world problems and hold promise for an equally unprecedented level of collaboration between actions and civic, public, and private sectors on the global stage.

Global investment needs are in the order of $5 trillion to $7 trillion per year. According to the UN Conference on Trade and Development, estimates for annual investment needs in developing countries alone range from $3.3 trillion to $4.5 trillion, mainly for basic infrastructure, roads, rails, ports, power stations, water, sanitation, food security, agriculture, rural development, climate change mitigation, adaption, health, and education at current levels of investment in SDG-relevant sectors. Developing countries alone based an annual gap of $2.5 trillion given the size of this gap and the role of the private sector investments will be indispensable. New online giving platforms such as Kickstarter have enabled more people. It gives you causes and organizations doing good work with which untapped potential remains to engage new donors and transform existing donors to be more strategic with their giving. The challenge for all mission-driven organizations that rely on donations is how to connect with these donors and engage them in a way that is simple and meaningful enough to ensure their long-term support for the world to succeed.

In 2014, the number of deaths in the United States grew by 23.9 percent compared to a 3.9 percent growth in private foundations, a 9.1 percent growth in lead trust, and a 5.7 percent growth in individual giving. In 2015, grants from donor-advised funds to charitable organizations reach a new high of $14.5 billion, $2 billion of that due to a 16.9 percent growth rate over 2014 grants. This popularity is largely due to the benefits afforded by the fiscal structure of decentralized applications (dApps), such as a 401k retirement account. The funds are eligible for immediate tax breaks and forming tax-free bridges to investments. How dApps can deepen foundation and charity engagement while maintaining a sustainable revenue stream is a fundamental challenge that affects every organization in the nonprofit sector.

The national philanthropic trusts found that these donors typically are more likely to attend events, sit on boards, and volunteer for the charities they support. They also tend to be more civically engaged and strategic about financial planning in general. These behaviors dovetail with the characteristics of a new generation of donors identified above. Attending social gatherings will increase many opportunities when meeting different people.

Proof

How does Madelyn engage House of Tiny Hands community during and after the COVID-19 pandemic? Any way she can. She doesn't view them as two separate events—life with COVID-19 and life without it—but rather as blanket coverage of how to reach people in every circumstance. This allows her and her staff to build a database of strategies that work, who they work on, and under what circumstances they work. Data becomes her new best friend, and while it will never replace the power of face-to-face conversations, it does deliver trend information, socioeconomic findings, and the ability to project how much to expect per quarter per demographic.

The pandemic made it essential for her organization to leave faxes and paper copies behind to cut expenses, and the results have been the marvelous integration of technology into their process. Their web portal, Facebook groups, social media followers, and a growing army of text and email subscribers make it much easier to proliferate their message than they ever dreamed possible. It's not the only weapon in her arsenal, though; Madelyn got this organization off the ground using good old-fashioned elbow grease, pounding the pavement and getting in front of the right people in the right situations. She continues to do that now as COVID-19 protocols start to recede and people are no longer afraid of a handshake or a public meeting. She's taking it step by step, not expecting a huge crowd to suddenly show up for a fancy soiree but hosting small get-togethers with refreshments and information. As tempting as it is to go to all points on the map right now and spread the charity's resources north, south, east, and west, she reminds herself that the number-one priority remains the Miami community, where it all started, and she's bound and determined to do right by it every single day of the year.

CHAPTER 6

Adversity

A dversity is at the heart of everything that nonprofit organizations are, if you really think about it. The focus of nonprofits is to overcome some adversity that some group of people is facing. Whether it's recovery from a hurricane; or fighting for a cure for a disease; or battling against something with a long shelf life such as educational inadequacy, prejudice, or a lack of tolerance, there's a fight going on somewhere that you have decided to get involved in. Likewise, every nonprofit faces adversity because they ask people to do something that most are not normally in the mindset of doing: giving their hard-earned money and not receiving something of tangible value in return. A person who can afford a Ferrari doesn't mind forking over $120,000 for it because they're getting a bright red sports car that can go 235 miles per hour in return! But when you ask someone who can barely afford a 1990 Toyota Tercel to give $100 in exchange for a tote bag or a bumper sticker and the feeling of helping out their community, that's where adversity starts to show itself.

ADVERSITY

My Story

I've discussed in the early chapters of this book how college life was for me. Over time, I've come to realize the biggest challenge wasn't coaches that didn't like me or a town that had inherent swathes of the population with a racist attitude toward a giant black kid roaming their malls and restaurants. No, the biggest challenge was my fear of failure. However, when life challenges you, you will either stand up to it or allow yourself to be sat down. I have learned over time that fear is a choice, and when I was playing offensive line, all I could do was remember to play fast and eventually the fear fell away. When I got to the NFL, the only adversity I imagined I would have been going up against guys with more experience and more moves than me, but I was confident that I would be able to overcome them with my constant dedication to the game, my capacity for improving my technique, and my ability to learn—I was very coachable, as the media likes to say. Of course, I could have never predicted the real adversity that I ended up dealing with—a life-threatening medical condition that momentarily ended my life and permanently ended my playing days.

Adversity can truly make you become someone you wouldn't have ever imagined being before facing adversity. I knew I would have to have a life after football, but I never imagined it would come so fast, so painfully, and via circumstances completely outside of my control. Fortunately, my approach, my mental preparedness, and my character allowed me to create a favorable outcome. When my body failed me, my mind was able to rebuild itself and prepare me to find new avenues to challenge myself and succeed. It took many repetitions to become stronger, fighting through the pain of rebuilding my body. When I realized I needed to become whole again, it changed my perspective. I forced myself to grow. There was no other choice. I knew one day I would get to become a successful businessman, but I would need to have a business and become my own boss.

Teachable Moments

The benefits of taking risks are far greater than the outcome of not taking a risk. Taking the risk means you're moving outside of the status quo. You're not content to do what you see being done around you and you're willing to be different for the sake of being better. Think of the big risks taken by the likes of Warren Buffett, Oprah Winfrey, Bill Gates, and Steve Jobs. Those people and thousands more like them decided that just being like everyone else wasn't going to be good enough for them; they needed to paint a bigger picture. Of course, not every risk is one worth taking. Calculated risks are the ones you need to pursue, when you've considered all the angles and done your homework and the rewards of success outweigh the threat of failure. You beat adversity by defining an objective. Then you begin implementing steps in your process to overtake it. No matter how big of a mountain there is in front of you, you can scale it if you take it step by step. Adversity will likely be there when you start your nonprofit. There will be some set of circumstances that keep you from enjoying success right away. But when you conquer that initial climb, you can't think that it will be smooth sailing for the rest of your time. Events like natural disasters, financial recessions, and, of course, the COVID-19 pandemic have a way of reorganizing our priorities and making us realize that there are always more challenges on the horizon; the question is how we take them on. I took a chance in pursuit of happiness and found passion chasing a dream.

Something attracted me to the financial industry and to the idea of helping people. That's what brought you to nonprofits as well: the challenge of creating your own lane, being able to change old ways, try new methods, and provide for others. You gain ground and then you go forward.

Proof

Madelyn knew adversity before she even knew how to talk. Born at 23 weeks and five days gestation, she had to be resuscitated and hooked up to a ventilator in her earliest days to keep her lungs going outside of the womb. When they took the first scans of her brain, doctors found a grade II and a grade IV brain bleed and weren't sure what they would result in. They later resulted in a low-grade form of cerebral palsy. At nine days of life, she suffered a perforated intestine that required a drain placed in her stomach to prevent further damage. In the first three months of her life, she had surgery to fix a tiny hole in her heart and another to prevent childhood blindness. A little thing like the COVID-19 pandemic didn't exactly shake her in her boots. However, she still had to work relentlessly to keep House of Tiny Hands afloat during the uncertain times. It couldn't be a blind rush, but rather a steady hand on the wheel. She had to prioritize what mattered the most to the nonprofit; she determined that meant letting the people that counted on her know that the COVID-19 pandemic was not the death knell of their services or their support.

Communication and a calming voice were everything in those early days, and she provided both to everyone in her circle—donors, employees, and the population they served—even when she wasn't feeling very calm or confident herself. From there, it was a matter of seeing what could be done, what was safe, and how to rally and galvanize a community that relied so heavily on personal interaction, smiles, and hugs, when suddenly all three were in short supply. What could have been an unmitigated disaster instead turned into the best thing that ever happened for Madelyn and the company.

CHAPTER 7

Leadership

eaders are not born; they are created when people accept and understand their strengths and weaknesses. You never know what you are until you experience a failure. That's when you make adjustments and start to build on what you could have done differently. If you follow that mindset, you develop into a leader, the kind of person that steps up to the challenge during adversity. You learn to combine critical thinking, common sense, and fearlessness. Leadership has a ton to do with being a decision-maker, but even more to do with taking the initiative instead of waiting for circumstances to present themselves to you.

ACCEPTANCE

My Story

I never wanted to be a leader on the football field. I was perfectly content to just be "one of the guys." I craved community and kinship in situations where I didn't stand out for any other reason than being tall and big. Even as a senior in high school, when I started getting looks from colleges all over the country, I was not the guy out there firing up the whole team before a matchup with a key rival. I was the best offensive lineman on the team and one of the best players, but I was doing my leading by example.

The same held true for much of my college career as a football player. I battled unpleasant coaches and new situations in the locker room and on the field, and while I really enjoyed my teammates, it took me a while to realize what was truly possible. I was so big and strong, even on a college football team, that people naturally gravitated toward me if I had something important to say.

One year, we whipped our rival in the biggest game of the year and I dominated their best player, putting him on the ground over and over. After the game, he and his teammates—and all of their female friends—showed up to party with us. He couldn't seem to stop running his mouth about how sorry we all were and finally I couldn't hear any more from him, so I stepped to him and cold-cocked him in front of everyone. It was a rare moment when I had all eyes on me that I wasn't wearing a helmet and pancaking someone, and the admiration and appreciation were palpable. I had seen a problem and decided to handle it by taking the initiative while everyone else was standing around waiting for something to happen.

Leaders step up to the challenge during adversity. Critical thinking, common sense, and fearlessness determine your success. Be a decision-maker and take the initiative to lead.

Teachable Moments

Leadership must make the best decisions, but if you don't inspire people or have their respect, being a great decision-maker is an after-thought. One of the best ways to be accepted as a leader is to have the humility to be open and allow your staff, your volunteers, and your donors to give you feedback. If you can't do anything but hear criticism when someone makes a suggestion or mentions an alternate way of doing things, then you're not being a leader, you're being a dictator. "Do as I say" might work when you're a parent or a military officer, but in the nonprofit world, where most people are working to contribute to a worthwhile cause, it's not going to go over well. You are the head of your organization, which generally means you've got significant experience and you're good at planning, but that doesn't mean you've got all of life's problems solved. If you're not transparent and approachable enough for your employees to be open with you, how can you expect them to take your direction in return? Some of the biggest parts of leadership involve picking another person to handle a situation. That requires trust that runs both ways. If you're not accepted as your organization's leader, you don't stand a chance.

Proof

Although she's a natural these days, Madelyn had her ups and downs at the beginning in getting accepted and respected as a leader. She was younger than all of her donors and most of her volunteers, but she often wore that inexperience on her face. She figured her calling card as a micro-preemie, the youngest ever to survive in the history of her hospital, would carry a lot of weight with most people. However, she learns that it might make for a good conversation starter at social events, but most people's knowledge of micro-preemies is limited, and she realizes it will be a lot tougher than it looks. So, she stops trying to impress everyone and instead is honest about who she is and why she started House of Tiny Hands. She admits that she doesn't know everything about micro-preemies from a medical perspective, but she is learning from every source she can. She admits that she doesn't have the best knowledge of how to run a nonprofit organization either, but she is going to be discussing all decisions with her senior staff members, that her door is always open, and that she wants suggestions on anything and everything whenever someone thinks they are on to something. In no short order, Madelyn establishes herself as affable, honest, and a great listener, all sensational qualities of a natural leader.

COMMON GOOD

My Story

One of the toughest things about being a leader of an organization is ensuring that successes and victories are shared by everyone on your team. The problem is that the local news station and the reporter from the paper don't have the time to interview 11 people, so they're just going to want the Big Cheese—that's you. Some people will start to see the charity and you as the same entity. Some people let this sort of power go to their heads. I was lucky that I didn't really know much about how the recruiting process for high school and college football works. If I had, I probably would have needed an extra pair of hands to carry my ego around my senior year of high school, when I was getting letters and phone calls from a ton of colleges all interested in having me play for them on an athletic scholarship.

When I was in college and starting to have a strong perfor- mance on the football field, there was an easy correlation between my success and the team's success. If I was the only one listening in the huddle, making adjustments based on the quarterback's call, and picking up blitzes, I might make all-conference, but the team would never move the ball, the quarterback would wind up in the emergency room, and the team would lose week after week. If I was able to help other guys in practice, help them pick up defensive formations, and develop such a rapport with the quarterback that he would trust I was protecting his blind side, then my success and the team's success would complement each other. When my effort helped everyone do well, the ripple effect was felt, from us converting more first downs, to getting more points, to more wins, to lighter practices, and from less-angry coaches to more looks from pro scouts at players on our squad. Team goals are a lot sweeter to achieve than individual ones because the feeling of community and the sharing of energy and emotion are magnified. Whenever I see a professional athlete take a giant contract with a not-so-good franchise, it tells me that leadership is not a priority. That remembered feeling is why I got into financial planning and then into helping nonprofits. My efforts are helping others succeed and I'm succeeding along with them. In those two roles, I was able to be a silent leader, which I really enjoyed. The companies and individuals I worked for reaped the benefits of my consultations.

Teachable Moments

Working together as a unit is not just important for team sports. Whether individuals might agree or disagree with your choices, team goals have to take the lead every time. The bigger picture of the organization has to remain top of mind. That includes something you might not be thinking about early in your leadership career, but something you need to address before too much time goes on: a succession plan for when you leave the organization, either to take a new role, to move to another industry, to spend more time with your family, or to retire—or due to tragic circumstances. Most entrepreneurs and startups often don't think about such scenarios, but preparing for all contingencies is necessary to ensure that the nonprofit goes on regardless of what happens at the top of the organization. You might not have anything more than the framework created, but there must be specifics in place for how a successor is chosen. Having such a plan in place is just another way to keep the focus on the common good, not on the individual.

Proof

Madelyn knows she'll need capable leaders if she's to expand nationwide, and that she will have to inherently trust them to do the right thing; nobody can be everywhere at once. Along with the board of directors, she begins constructing a program to follow for qualifying, interviewing, and vetting new leadership, including for her own position. She doesn't want to think about the day she leaves House of Tiny Hands behind, but when it comes, she wants it to be cared for by the very best person possible. This includes approval from a majority of the board of directors, knowledge of the lives of micro-preemies, and strong empathy skills for dealing with mothers who have had and lost tiny babies.

IMPACT

My Story

When you're six feet, seven inches tall and tip the scales at more than 300 pounds, it's pretty simple to make an impact on someone. When I was at my best on the football field, that impact lasted more than a few hours on some guys. When I started working with nonprofits, I knew that I had to make a different sort of impact, one that would not only improve its fortunes in the now, but would also give it the opportunity to keep that cycle perpetuating long after I had gone on to my next consulting job. It was straight out of the old parable about giving a man a fish versus teaching a man to fish. As great as it is to lead an organization, when your goal is to make that community as strong as possible for as long as possible, you need to make your impact long-lasting.

When I got into financial planning, I made my plan of attack equal parts advice and education. I can take a look at someone's finances and see how they move their money around and what avenues of investment to take in order to maximize their return, but most people don't want to employ a financial planner for the next 30 years to keep asking for more help from. That's why I take care of people in the moment and then try to impart as much wisdom on them as possible, so they can make their own best decisions going forward. The same holds true when I advise nonprofits on how best to move forward, particularly during COVID-19. The job is to help them immediately and also teach them to help themselves. The old fisherman concept again. I tell clients that I know I've done a good job if they never call me again, except to say thanks!

Teachable Moments

How do you impact your nonprofit from the inside out? For starters, you roll up your sleeves and get dirty at the forefront of the problem your charity is addressing. You put your body to work, do some of the day-to-day activities, and show that even in tough, challenging times, there is no job too big or too small. When you go on the site of an event, show up with creative ideas in mind, hand out bottles of water, whatever it takes to get involved. It's not just about showing up, it's about establishing yourself as someone people want to like and want to believe in. If you can provide the proper motivation, people won't be likely to quit on you when the going gets tough. Having an impact means going beyond what is expected. It means helping staff members out with a grocery bill or a mortgage when times are tough, and the pandemic makes you cut hours. Understand that the open hand is stronger than the closed fist when it comes to leaving a lasting impact on your charges and your staff. You want to involve as many people as possible in the mix of your organization; this goes back to our discussions about diversification and culture. The more types of people with more backgrounds and cultures, the more experiences you can draw from to get the best possible solution to every problem. You always want to add people who can bring in new ideas and are not afraid to open up.

Proof

Madelyn's gift for public speaking is not a prerequisite for future leaders of House of Tiny Hands. She goes out of her way to find different types of leaders—those that are whizzes on social media, or those from different socioeconomic settings that give them credibility with women of different races, religions, and income levels. She seeks out anyone who can make an impact on the population segments that are impacted by micro-preemies and begins training them up for leadership roles. When the COVID-19 pandemic starts to wane, she turns her considerable assets of social media and messaging over to the disposal of the state to help get people vaccinated, explaining it in terms of how it works, how it will not affect a baby, and how getting it helps women stay safe and gives them the opportunity to live a long, healthy life as mothers to their children—present and future.

CHAPTER 8

Obstacles

I n life, facing obstacles will either break you or make you stronger. Figuring out how to take on obstacles is all in your mentality. Deciding to give up, to avoid them, or to continue pursuing your objective is a cultivated talent that you must focus on daily in order to make the right moves when the time comes.

INJURED

My Story

Every athlete suffers injuries. A sprained ankle. A torn ligament. Jammed fingers and cracked ribs. My career-ending injury went beyond that. It threatened my life. Heck, it took my life for a couple of minutes before doctors were able to bring me back. There has never been a bigger obstacle in my entire life than the blood clots that had me within inches of being dead for good or having my leg amputated, meaning I would certainly never play football again and only walk with the aid of artificial means. People often say a darkness falls on them when they suffer a traumatic injury. For me, that darkness was a literal one, as my life seemed to go dark from the time I was taken in the ambulance, through the surgery, and into recovery when I woke up surrounded by family members who loved me.

I didn't particularly know it at the time but seeing them all surrounding me was the catalyst to how I was going to move forward in life. They were all there to take care of me, and that was something that I knew a lot about—taking care of people. The light bulb seemed to go off when I thought back to that moment, realizing that helping people was every bit as important, if not more so, as football was. I started by getting a job to support my own family. I wasn't trying to get back into football, nor was I trying to do some sort of miracle recovery. I wanted to stay grounded and start putting my life back together one step at a time. I was able to fall back on my business training and get right into a career that focused my mind and gave me the opportunity to put money in the bank. I wasn't trying to change the world in one day, just get through each day and make the next one better.

Teachable Moments

When an organization gets injured, everyone feels it: leadership, staff, volunteers, donors, the population you're looking out for, and everyone's families, as well. Injuries to organizations can come in a large variety of forms: a loss of funding, a loss of staff, misuse of funds, supporting something controversial and having backlash from a group, negative media coverage, or even a pandemic that shuts down your way of doing things. It's never easy to suffer a setback with your organization because when you're trying to raise money and make life better for a group of people, you don't expect negatives to crop up. But when you do run afoul of obstacles—

internal or external, you need to not try to fix everything all at once. Life doesn't work that way, and neither will your organization. Recognizing obstacles and dealing with them requires planning and patience, not rashness and snap decisions. Remember, this is not just your obstacle; it belongs to everyone in your organization and mishandling it can lead to disaster. While charities often thrive on emotions, dealing with obstacles requires a lack of them in most cases. Using your head is preferable by far to letting your heartstrings tug on your decisions. If the obstacle in question is that a 10-year employee who was one of your original employees has been caught stealing funds from the company, it's not time to listen to your heart and give them another chance. Sound business practices require sound business decisions. Make sure you take them slowly and methodically to stay on the path to recovery.

Proof

House of Tiny Hands suffers a dramatic loss of donations during the early months of the COVID-19 pandemic. No one is sure what the future holds for the US economy, but people are losing their jobs left and right, the stock market is in freefall for weeks, and the idea of donating money seems laughable to most people. CEO Madelyn doesn't know when or where things will bottom out any more than anyone else does, but she knows that surviving it is the charity's top priority. She goes to the board of directors and requests permission to access the emergency fund in order to keep her staff's payroll intact on a month-by-month basis and keep funding programs at local hospitals for mothers of micro-preemies. Right now, there is not a long-term solution because there isn't enough information. But pulling the programs or cutting staff seems like a panic move and inciting a panic at a time like this doesn't make any sense to Madelyn or her board.

RECOVERY

My Story

After surgery, I didn't even try walking for weeks and I lost about 70 pounds in the hospital. How's that for leaving there a changed man? It wasn't a change I wanted, but when I was finally strong enough, I left the hospital to start my recovery. At first, all this meant was doing basic things the same way each day to relearn what normal living even was. I'm talking about brushing my teeth, getting dressed, breathing exercises, meditation, remembering my gratitudes, and so forth—the kinds of things I wouldn't even think about needing to do in an earlier life. Now I had to be methodical with each and every one of them, each and every day. If I didn't, I risked falling into depression, refusing to get out of bed, and wallowing in self-pity about the end of my football career and the huge task of getting back into shape that I now faced.

I had to focus on the first thing, which was learning how to take care of myself again. It was a hard fact of life that I had been on my own since leaving for college, had traveled all over North America chasing my football dream, and now things like buttoning my pants and taking a shower required assistance. Taking those next tentative steps to establishing what was going to be my process required a lot of focus on my part. Since high school, I had been doing different versions of the same routine on a daily basis. Over time, my diet was geared toward being an offensive lineman. So was my weight-lifting routine, my other fitness activities, the amount of sleep I got, what I studied on film, and when I left for practice and how long I stayed. Now all of those things were over and done with, forever. What was next? Where did I apply all that energy? When you play any sport or have a consistent exercise routine, hydration is critical. I was massively dehydrated when I was taken to the emergency room. My body had stopped working correctly and I didn't realize it until I simply could not function any longer.

Teachable Moments

When you face obstacles in your nonprofit, quick fixes are rarely the solution. Slapping a bandage on a problem or putting your finger in the leak isn't going to stop the problem, it will probably just delay it until it comes up again. Obstacles will test the limit of how well you can multitask and delegate authority because you can't simply stop all operations of your organization when a problem arises; you have to keep pushing forward with all your other plans while solving the problem at hand. That means putting the focus on the problem without disrupting the day-to-day of your operation and the focus of its employees.

If you have three people doing marketing for you and there's suddenly a need to fix a digital campaign that isn't reaching its financial goals or has drawn criticism from your donors; you can't pull all three team members off their assignments to focus on just one thing. You need to focus on dividing up your time between current projects and the obstacle in order to return it to the status quo while still moving forward with your other goals. Even when the pandemic hit in 2020, some parts of your organization still needed to operate as is. Your call center, your bookkeeping, your staff applying for grants from the government—they all keep moving forward to keep the boat on the right course while you find ways to remove those obstacles from your path. Keep doing the things that work in your organization. Put them on repeat and don't stray from the path that is working for you. If you are having budget problems, focus on things that can be trimmed from your financial spending to get leaner.

And hydration isn't just for athletes. You need to refuel your organization's energy and motivation from time to time if you're going to be in this for the marathon that it is. That doesn't mean everyone needs to start drinking Gatorade around the office. It does mean that you need to be open to new ideas. Don't keep secrets about your charity's struggles from your staff. The cause belongs to everyone, no matter how much responsibility you might carry as its leader. Give everyone a heads up about what obstacle is in your way and give them all the opportunity to contribute to a solution. Look elsewhere for solutions as well; not every problem can be solved solely by your knowledge base! Reach out to professional resources, see what other nonprofits are doing in similar circumstances, take online classes in the field you are lacking, and scout the internet for videos, webinars, and other solutions that will give you inspiration without costing you hundreds or thousands of dollars to gain access to.

Proof

Madelyn is not above her own pride and ego when it comes to getting House of Tiny Hands back on track as COVID-19 wears on and on. She fixes her daily news feeds on nonprofits and how they are coping with the lack of social interaction and economic uncertainty. When she sees ideas that capture her attention, she makes notes and sends them around in memo emails to her senior staff, wanting their feedback. She's not going to start following every stray lead, but she knows that the nonprofit cannot survive long-term by bleeding through its emergency fund. Creative steps will have to be taken and soon. With the quarantine making her daily trips to the office a luxury that she can't really afford, she works from home and finds the environment allows for more free time. She uses this to take webinars and online courses on financial planning, crisis planning, and other topics that are timely. Zoom calls with other nonprofit leaders and even a few celebrity ones give her extra insight into steps that can be made now that the pandemic is here and everyone is struggling equally.

CHAPTER 9

Going After It

When you have done all your homework and research, manifested your dreams and goals into writing, and assembled a staff around you that you think can weather the storm and future storms as well, it's time to flip the switch, fire up the engine, and pursue the dreams of getting your nonprofit back on the playing field and making the transition from good to great. That clear vision of what you want the world to look like might not ever become reality, but your goal is to get it as close to perfect as possible.

PLANNING

My Story

Football was my focus for a long time; but if you recall, just before pursuing my NFL dreams, I was at a fork in the road between trying for the league and going on a one-year internship in China for business school. I had put the internship away to focus on football, but that didn't mean I wasn't talented enough work in the business field; you don't get a master's degree without a lot of intent and effort. As the rebuilding of my body and my functionality progressed, my family and I talked about the grim reality of the state of our finances, and I realized we had a common goal. I needed to refocus my life on something that didn't involve draw plays and pass protection and we needed a reliable source of income.

The two goals combined into one: I used my education and college experience to land a good job that paid me a steady salary, let me flex my mental muscles rather than my physical ones, and didn't require me to go through two-a-day practices every August. It was a very different environment straight off the bat. College was a few years in my past at that point. I had been with the Dolphins for a season, then in Canada, and then in Pennsylvania, where the blood clots happened. Getting into a day-to-day business environment, wearing a suit instead of shoulder pads, and leaving when the clock said 5 p.m. rather than when a coach decided we'd done enough shuttle runs and one-on-one drills were all new things for me.

Naturally, I made some mistakes along the way. I was behind on the lingo of the business environment and had to catch up. I was used to straightforward talk from coaches who would look you in the eye and tell you to your face if they thought you were doing great or terrible. Not everyone told the truth in my new industry, and some people would smile at your face while sharpening the knife to put in your back. So, like a kid driving alone the day after getting their license, I plotted a bumpy course—but I did get on the road and start moving.

Teachable Moments

When you have your business plan set up and have that goal in mind, whether it's at the beginning of your nonprofit's existence, after you've hit an obstacle, or when you're getting back to full strength following a major interruption such as the pandemic, you need to make it the vision for everyone—staff, volunteers, donors, and your target audience. Whether it's raising $50,000 for a cause, educating the public on a specific need, or getting a law passed or changed, giving that vision commonality is the way to focus all available energies on it. It makes everyone work more cohesively, as well, knowing there's an objective that they all share—from the CEO at the top of the food chain to the volunteer who just signed up online last night.

That unity is essential to achieving goals that last beyond the end of the work week. Life happens for everyone, and regardless of how dedicated a staffer is, they are still going to be at least equally focused on their own lives, families, hobbies, and interests. Getting them locked in on the mission while they're in the work environment is essential to get their maximum effort and contribution. No one's goal is going to be perfect, and much like my foray back into the business world, you and your staff are going to make mistakes along the way. That's to be expected, and if they're unintentional, you certainly shouldn't beat yourself or anyone else up about them. Learning from them is crucial; never brush aside a mistake as a fluke or a once-in-a-lifetime occurrence. There's value to be learned in everything.

Proof

As 2022 dawns, Madelyn's goal for House of Tiny Hands crystallizes. She'll spend half of the year guiding the original Miami location and training her successor and the other half traveling the state and the nation to help start other locations of the nonprofit, putting together staffs and boards of directors, setting up networks with local healthcare organizations, and performing speaking engagements for politicians and chambers of commerce to get the donation ball rolling in the right direction. It will be grueling work, and it will require her senior staff to take on new responsibilities and be more proactive when it comes to decision-making, but she knows they can handle it. There will be mistakes made both in Miami and as she moves around the country, but she believes every one of them will be a learning experience that makes the next project that much stronger.

PURSUIT

My Story

I chased football excellence on the professional level for a long time. I felt like my momentum was at an all-time high going into that Steelers' training camp. I was wrong. Building momentum again after you've had a huge letdown is one of the toughest things to do in life, regardless of what profession you're in, who you are, where you live, or what your goal is. For me, it started with simple things. Taking care of myself, putting my faith in God that things were going to get better, doing my rehab exercises faithfully, and feeling myself get stronger. Football was in the past, but it had never been my only dream, and I knew that I could get motivated to go after other goals. That positive attitude started influencing my decisions. I got my resume in order. I reached out to people from business school and let them know my situation. I educated myself on what sorts of jobs were available and I started getting my name out there. I had to dig deep to find the winning attitude that I had cultivated during high school and college. Losing a part of yourself will do that to you. I won't pretend there weren't some dark hours during that time, when I questioned why I could get so close to fulfilling my dream and then have it taken away. But the past is the past and nobody can change it; I knew that there was a way forward to achieve my dreams and I was determined to take it.

Teachable Moments

If you feel like COVID-19 disrupted your momentum and put you back at square one, there are two things to understand. The first is that you are not alone. In fact, if your nonprofit is still alive and kicking, you're doing a lot better than tons of organizations around the country. According to Candid[4], in a normal year as many as 12,000 charities will go out of business across the US. In 2020, the number when all the dust settled was thought to be as many as 120,000. Your plan for a new start begins today, with you deciding what you want the future to look like and beginning to put that plan in motion. All of the little decisions you're making on a day-to-day basis are building toward greatness down the road. It might not feel like you're doing much at the moment—exploring social media options, putting out flyers for volunteers, or cold-calling donors to start establishing a level of rapport—but these small moves create momentum.

Think of yourself standing behind a boulder and pushing it forward a little at a time. It will be very difficult at first and you might only roll it forward an inch or two, but each little push makes the next little push that much easier and makes the boul-

---

4   Jacob Harold, "How many nonprofits will shut their doors?," Candid., July 15, 2020, https://blog.candid.org/post/how-many-nonprofits-will-shut-their-doors/.

der roll that much farther. After a bunch of pushes, it starts to move on its own from the potential energy you're building up, and before you know it, it's running over the competition and making an impact wherever it goes. The small steps get magnified as the process goes on. Putting as much care and effort into the small decisions as you do into the big ones is essential to building a new foundation for your nonprofit to start growing on. Little by little, the steps you are taking will begin opening new doors and making new connections, getting you in touch with people that will give you the opportunity to effect change on a larger scale. The little steps are essential to your momentum, and they are also a sort of practice for seeing how you function, what you do best, how your staff work together, how they work apart, and how to maximize everyone's efforts at the same time toward the same result. It can be done.

Proof

With the aid of her staff, volunteers, donors, and the board of directors, Madelyn has a plan in place to rebuild House of Tiny Hands brick by brick following the COVID-19 pandemic. Little setbacks get magnified in the moment. When her organization doesn't move forward in a grant process or when an exciting candidate for a position opts to take a corporate job instead of coming on board, it's easy to get down and out. But Madelyn's faith has carried her through dark times before, and she knows it can be done again. The world has changed, and she must change with it in order to keep her nonprofit growing and thriving, just the same as the doctors charged with getting micro-preemies to do the same thing under similar circumstances.

Momentum will come in unexpected places: When the charity trends on social media for its innovative marketing slogan one day.

When a favorite donor decides to make a statement that it's time for Miami to start giving again and drops off a check for $5,000 one afternoon. This momentum will fuel Madelyn's decision and next steps. As a leader, it is her job to harness it and make sure that energy spreads through her staff as well. As their good decisions mount, anything starts to seem possible again.

EXECUTION

My Story

When I finished my first year as a financial planner, I was so busy and so joyful, I almost didn't recognize the significance of the calendar. It was an accomplishment I was proud of, of course, but the fact that I had found something to get passionate about made the time move quickly and kept me from dwelling on the "what ifs" of my life too often. My action plan to use my passion and my qualifications for business was in full effect; I was smiling daily, making new friends and connections, and helping people. Things were going well, and I was already trending toward nonprofits, knowing that they were making the biggest 1:1 community impact, and I wanted in, using my skill set to help them on their own journeys. Of course, I was still making mistakes, but like when they called me that "coachable" offensive lineman, I was open to feedback anywhere and any way I could get it. I never had a problem with someone telling me what I could be doing better because doing better is what life is all about. If you're perfect on day one, what are you going to be for the rest of the time? Very bored.

Teachable Moments

Your action plan should feel like a living, breathing document. It's going to change over time as your circumstances change. Don't be so fixated on what your plan says that you're missing what's right in front of you. If your plan calls for five new volunteers to be recruited every month, don't send the other five home when 10 show up to your open house. If your Twitter hashtag doesn't trend in the first week of use, don't throw it on the trash heap and try something else—give it room to breathe and figure out a way to make your message more engaging. Most of all, take any and all feedback you can get—from your staff, from the public, from any third party you do business with, literally anyone. Even the people who are negative about you will give you information you previously didn't have; how you use it is up to you. Keep feeding new data back into your brain trust and analyze how to make the future better for your charity and for the people it serves. And when you do reach accomplishments—goals met for donations, work anniversaries for your staff, the number of volunteers recruited—celebrate like you've won the Super Bowl, because in many ways you have. Anything a nonprofit can do to make lives better is a joyous, powerful accomplishment. Make sure your staff, volunteers, and donors always know exactly how amazing they are and how much you appreciate their contributions.

Proof

It takes six weeks longer than the business plan calls for, but Madelyn has successfully gotten the second location of House of Tiny Hands up and running in Mobile, Alabama. A full-time staff of three is out now, recruiting volunteers and pounding the pavement at hospitals and community centers to find the people who will carry their message forward. Back at home, Madelyn is working hand in hand with her eventual replacement, Lily, another micro-preemie turned activist who is passionate about animals and people and has a smile that can light up a room. Madelyn has told Lily that she hopes to have her installed as the local CEO by the second quarter of 2023. The younger woman feels like she'll never be ready, but Madelyn reminds her that's what being a micro-preemie is all about: getting to your destination ahead of schedule.

CHAPTER 10

The End of the Beginning

would be lying if I said I don't wonder from time to time what life would have looked like if I hadn't suffered my career-ending injuries all those years ago. Say I had impressed at the Steelers' training camp and made the team. It would have meant playing for a storied franchise in NFL history with incredible Hall of Fame talent and coaches. If I had stayed in the league for a few years, I would have been worth millions for playing a game I loved. After my career ended, I might have hung around the game as a coach, an analyst, or a front office guy. It would have been a great life. But God always has a plan, doesn't He? And His plan for me was to get me off the field for good, so I couldn't have any lingering doubts about whether I had another shot left in me. He made it abundantly obvious that those days were over, and I needed to get on with the rest of my life.

And what a life it's been since then! I have met people from a wide, diverse spectrum of passions, races, and places. I have been able to help businesses and nonprofits grow beyond their current limitations, find the resources and techniques to widen their net for attracting donors, and make a much more significant impact than they previously thought possible. Working with charities allows me to see the best part of what the human experience is and, while it might sound like a cliche, it consistently shows me the very best of myself, as well.

Nonprofits overwhelmingly begin from a place of hope and help. They fail for any number of reasons, but a failure to apply proper business and financial strategies is consistently the number-one problem. I wish I could say that simply wanting to do good in the world is enough of a reason to succeed as a charity, but that is a myopic, misguided ideal that the real world cannot possibly live up to. Nonprofits need help, and it's my job to give it to as many of them as I can. The smiling faces, the tears of joy, the radiance of hope that nonprofits deliver to people regardless of their race, religion, gender, or creed is one of the most powerful forms of giving that this world has ever known.

You can push past your current obstacles—be they struggle with donors, inability to plan financially, or fighting back to solvency post-COVID-19. The answers are out there; you can acquire them if you know where to start looking. Remember, it can be done. The lessons, tools, and tips you have seen in the pages of this book are yours to use as you see fit to turn your own nonprofit into the biggest success possible. Take what you like and leave the rest, as they say. I am hopeful that you have found motivation, inspiration, and dedication in the pages of this text to take your nonprofit to the next level as the world gets back to doing business in the post-pandemic era. These are the basics, the building blocks that will form the cornerstones of your nonprofit and allow you to start aiming toward the sky and all you can accomplish.

When you've built your base and you're ready to take the next step toward long-term nonprofit success, check out my next book and we'll continue this wonderful journey together!

ACKNOWLEDGMENTS

To everyone who has participated on my journey on building the steppingstones and helping me with my first book has truly inspired me to become a published author.

I'd like to thank GOD, family, and my team and all the support who have entered my life during the right time and who have also offered me the opportunity to learn and become more enthusiastic about writing my book.

I'd like to thank Ken Dunn for providing a perspective and clearly empathizing how to become the authority of my industry and motivated me to take the risk and become a successful published author.

I'd like to thank my team at Morgan James Publishing for all the support and guidance in preparation of publishing my first book it was just an amazing team of individuals with great ideas and a clear strategy with the overall experience which was comfortable and encouraging to have an organization walk you through step-by-step how to complete publishing a book.

I'd like to also thank my editors for helping me with getting organized providing their expertise and helping to polish up my story!

Pastor Bruce Hogan has always been truthful, somebody who's been inspiring and motivating to always encouraged me to pursue my goals and my dreams but always a man of faith and with teaching has implanted me with wisdom to place God first in my life.

Brother Bryson is like a big brother and always encouraged me to become great and continue to follow my passions, he inspired the teachings and motivated my belief that God created everything and always makes the impossible become possible.

Coach Keynodo Hudson has made a tremendous impact in my life and has always encouraged me not to be complacent. He inspired me to utilize my talents for the best opportunities as a football player. He would always repeat words in the locker room and on the practice field and even in the weight room that the "good become great and the great become unstoppable" and those words never left my mind. Those words were an inspiration to never quit and continue pushing myself through with hard work and dedication.

Tony Thomas is a world-class trainer who pushed me, challenge me, and made me compete and without those workout sessions adding fuel to my fire. You transformed my game on and off the field and have been such an impactful person in my life.

Damien Stevens a motivational trainer that help push me to new limits. You're consistent coaching and dedication towards my success help improve my flexibility and my mobility. You also became a good friend and a great mentor.

THANK YOU

Thank you God, my family, coaches, mentors, friends, and all the readers who have read the book. I inspire you to continue your efforts and never give up.

My appreciation and gratitude to you for reading the book and learning more about my story has allowed me to continue to thrive and focus on providing more value in the next edition.

You have entered my journey and understood more of who I am personally, professionally, and philanthropically.

Pastor Bruce Hogan and brother Lawrence Bryson Sr. are two special individuals who were there for me during my years at university and they both encouraged me to grow my connection with God.

I admire these gentlemen who have been amazing mentors and have always been there for me in the most challenging times, from adversity to traumatic injuries and at the hospital when I faced my near-death experience.

In the next edition, we're going to dive into more case studies and the experiences of nonprofit organizations to gain a deeper dive in to how they have applied some of the strategies and gather the inside scoop and data from the response as to where of the conversation and where legacy planning evolves perpetually.

For those of you who recommend my book to other communities, you will receive a gift. We will be sending you a discount coupon for my next edition simply by typing in your email and your information. This will allow me to send you a coupon, which is a discount code for the next edition.

I ask that you continue to come along the journey and recommend *Let's Get It* to a friend or family or nonprofit organization that you believe in.

For a quicker response and feedback here are my handles on social media:

- Facebook: KrisDouraFinance
- Instagram: zoe_the_legend
- Twitter: @DouraKristoffer
- LinkedIn: KristofferDoura
- info@kristofferdoura.com
- www.KristofferDoura.com

Stay tuned and fasten your seatbelts. You're going to be in for a special treat and much more to come.....

ABOUT THE AUTHOR

Living my second best life each and every day!

Kristoffer's life is a journey and living in Miami, Florida is a major blessing in a way that he thrives living in great weather and surrounding himself with amazing people from different cultures and diversity. This is the reason for his success and ability to become great.

The truth is location, the sunlight, the green trees, and the blue ocean waves are what inspire him to want to live his life in peace in the tropical weather of South Beach.

As a financial professional and philanthropist, the expertise that he has obtained throughout his professional career has been focused and concentrated on nonprofit, legacy, and business succession planning.

Kristoffer has taken the responsibility at the Families First of Palm Beach County as a Board of Directors and Committee Chairman of Legacy Gifts as a volunteer. He loves getting his hands dirty and participating in volunteer work and making time and dedicating energy toward the greater good which truly makes him feel inspired.

Some of the types of work he does do in the community evolves around helping kids, parents, and organizations with missions that are very close and dear to his heart such as organizations like, Symphony of Palm Beach, Boys and Girls Club Broward County, Hugs and Smiles, and Big Brothers Big Sisters Miami and that inspires participation helping the community and the organizations in throughout the Florida region.

Doura stated, "It feels amicable to help drive my focus to get involved and get experience on all levels of engagement."

As he continues his life journey, Kristoffer is an eligible bachelor and focuses on having great health, mind, and spirit, which are very important for his personal growth. He enjoys reading, cooking, musical instruments traveling, and growing his understanding of what life truly offers outside of his comfort zone.

A free ebook edition is available with the purchase of this book.

To claim your free ebook edition:

1. Visit MorganJamesBOGO.com
2. Sign your name CLEARLY in the space
3. Complete the form and submit a photo of the entire copyright page
4. You or your friend can download the ebook to your preferred device

A **FREE** ebook edition is available for you or a friend with the purchase of this print book.

CLEARLY SIGN YOUR NAME ABOVE

Instructions to claim your free ebook edition:
1. Visit MorganJamesBOGO.com
2. Sign your name CLEARLY in the space above
3. Complete the form and submit a photo of this entire page
4. You or your friend can download the ebook to your preferred device

Print & Digital Together Forever.

Snap a photo

Free ebook

Read anywhere

CPSIA information can be obtained
at www.ICGtesting.com
Printed in the USA
JSHW081559010523
41092JS00001B/77